P9-CQB-916

KNITTINGNATURE

39 DESIGNS INSPIRED BY PATTERNS IN NATURE

NORAH GAUGHAN

photographs by **Thayer Allyson Gowdy**
photostyling by **Karen Schaupeter**

STC CRAFT | A MELANIE FALICK BOOK

STEWART, TABORI & CHANG
NEW YORK

For my parents, Phoebe Adams Gaughan and Jack Gaughan,
who lovingly raised me to appreciate both art and science.

Text copyright © 2006 Norah Gaughan
Photographs except page 148 copyright © 2006 Thayer Allyson Gowdy
Photograph on page 148 courtesy of Getty Images.

The following companies generously provided props, wardrobe, and accessories for
the *Knitting Nature* photos:
Still Life
  The Gardener, 1836 Fourth Street, Berkeley, CA 94710, www.thegardener.com
  The Bone Room, 1569 Solano Avenue, Berkeley, CA 94707, www.boneroom.com
Wardrobe and Accessories
  Macy's West, 170 O'Farrell Street, San Francisco, CA 94102, www.macys.com
  Zilda by Flavia, 340 Bryant Street, Studio 102, San Francisco, CA 94107, www.zildabyflavia.com
  House of Hengst Inc., 924 Valencia Street, San Francisco, CA 94110, www.houseofhengst.com
  Painted Bird, 1201A Guerrero Street, San Francisco, CA 94110, www.paintedbird.org

Published in 2006 by
Stewart, Tabori & Chang
An imprint of Harry N. Abrams Inc.

Library of Congress Cataloging-in-Publication Data
Gaughan, Norah.
    Knitting Nature : 39 designs inspired by patterns in nature / Norah Gaughan ; photographs by
        Thayer Allyson Gowdy.—1st ed.
        p. cm.
    Includes index.
    ISBN 1-58479-484-4
    1. Knitting—Patterns. 2. Knitwear. I. Title

    TT825.G28 2006
    746.43'2041—dc22
    2005026722

Edited by Melanie Falick

Book Design: Anna Christian
Production Manager: Jane Searle

The text of this book was composed in Minion and Gotham.

Printed in China
10 9 8 7 6 5 4 3 2 1

HNA
harry n. abrams, inc.
a subsidiary of La Martinière Groupe
115 West 18th Street
New York, NY 10011
www.hnabooks.com

CONTENTS

FOREWORD

I am extremely pleased and honored to introduce Norah Gaughan's first book. Norah and I have been friends for nearly two decades—longer than either of us like to think about. Our respective views of the world overlap to a remarkable degree. How, in the early part of the twenty-first century, can an artist and a scientist find so much intellectual common ground? Some clues to the answer to this question can be found in *Knitting Nature*, which explores the use of naturally occurring geometrical motifs in knitting.

Over the years, Norah and I have had numerous discussions regarding the duality between patterns in nature and patterns in knitting. Our talks have ranged over many topics, particularly the powerful unifying role of symmetry principles, which govern the behavior of physical systems on all scales. Several of Norah's highly original designs are illustrative of this principle and incorporate aspects of hexagonal and pentagonal symmetries, the latter making contact with nonperiodic tilings of the plane and other modern developments. Another topic we have discussed is the emergence of complex behaviors from seemingly simple rules in systems such as the Koch curve. Norah has made use of this concept in her design of the Coastline Camisole and Skirt as well as in my favorite, the elegant Ogee Tunic. In each of these examples, Norah's clear and beautifully written descriptions reflect her deep understanding of the underlying scientific principles.

On a more abstract note, Norah and I have often wondered about the possible applications of mathematics to knitting. It is known that there is a surprisingly sophisticated and subtle mathematical theory of certain aspects of knitting. Cable patterns are related to mathematical objects known as braid groups. Likewise, the problem of optimally picking up stitches is connected to solving systems of so-called Diophantine equations. The eighteenth-century philosopher Immanuel Kant famously declared that the criterion for the development of a true science lies in its relation to mathematics. Evidently, one lesson to be learned from *Knitting Nature* is that a similar criterion may apply to some forms of art. In his classic work, *The Structure of Scientific Revolutions*, Thomas Kuhn introduced the concept of the paradigm shift—an intellectual revolution in which one world view is replaced by another. It may not be an exaggeration to suggest that *Knitting Nature* accomplishes such a transformation.

It has been somewhat facetiously said that it is difficult to make predictions, especially about the future. Nevertheless, I expect that the impact of Norah's ideas will be widely felt within the knitting community. Perhaps one of the readers of this book will be inspired to further explore the connections between knitting and the natural world and thereby extend Norah's pioneering vision.

Prof. John C. Schotland
University of Pennsylvania

INTRODUCTION

'd be overdramatizing if I were to say that I've led a double life since childhood. But there is a kernel of truth to it—I have always been torn between simultaneous desires to study art and science. I grew up in a household of artists. Both of my parents were commercial illustrators; Dad specialized in science fiction and Mom in technical illustrations of domestic endeavors such as gardening and sewing. In our family we made art all the time. A favorite after-dinner game was separately drawing the body parts of fanciful creatures—one person would do the head, another the body, and another the legs—and then combining the parts to hilarious and clever effect. At Christmas my brother and I made elaborate ornaments with Mom and printed our own linoleum-block Christmas cards with Dad. When it came to school projects, our household held resources rivaled by none—paints, papers, clay, wood, and fabric, all within easy reach. Early on I learned about needle arts from my maternal grandmother, who lived with us, as well as from my mother. I crocheted first, creating mostly elaborate vests and drawstring bags with Clorox-bottle bottoms. I also embroidered and sewed. No one in the house knit, but a friend taught me when I was fourteen. Knitting immediately became my medium of choice.

I was good at art and liked it. In school, however, I loved science and math. At Brown University, I intended to focus on biology, but in my junior year, perhaps a bit homesick, I started taking art classes. I ended up with an undergraduate degree in biology with a concentration in studio art. In the high schools and colleges in the 1970s and 1980s, we girls were strongly encouraged (and for good reason) to pursue previously male-dominated fields. While the attitude that women can do anything was definitely a positive influence, it was accompanied by an underlying attitude of condescension toward traditional feminine work. When I ended up pursuing a career in knitting after college, I had to fight a voice in myself that continued to tell me that knitting wasn't a serious enough endeavor.

I had dabbled in sweater design while in high school, publishing an early piece through my mother's contacts in the needlework industry. Over the next few years, similar contacts provided a bit more work. After college, I joined the thriving knitting community in Providence, which included the renowned designers Margery Winter and Deborah Newton. Gradually I realized that knitting for a living could make me happy and scrapped any ideas I had about pursuing science professionally. Deborah generously recommended editors for me to contact for design work and Margery actually taught me how to design. I have always looked upon this very busy period as my own version of graduate school. Since those early days in Providence, I've probably designed over a thousand garments for magazines, books, and yarn companies. I've also designed stitch patterns for ready-to-wear, worked for fashion designer Adrienne Vittadini, and spent several years as the design director at JCA, a major American handknitting yarn company. I am now the design director at Berroco Yarns, where I am once again happily collaborating with Margery Winter, the company's creative director.

The work in this book feels like the melding of my science- and art-loving selves, as well as the continuation of themes that have been developing in my work for years. My favorite part of knitting has always been conquering new challenges. At first this meant making up new twisted stitches and cable patterns. Then, a few years ago, the challenge became experimenting with nontraditional garment construction—thinking beyond the normal front, back, and sleeves construction (for instance, using circles as building blocks for garments) and discovering new ways to knit garments from side to side or in one piece. My many years of experience gave me the skills and confidence to explore uncharted territory. So I was ready when I tripped across the idea for this book. While perusing the popular-science section in the local bookshop, I picked up *The Self-Made Tapestry*, an introduction to pattern formation in nature written by physicist Philip Ball. The visuals drew me in and as I read, I became fascinated with Ball's demonstrations of how nature's patterns appear again and again in situations that are seemingly unrelated. Similar patterns are made by different processes because, ultimately, only a few laws of physics control growth and form. For instance, spirals and branches are two of the core shapes found in organic and inorganic patterns all around us. Spirals are seen in circumstances as diverse as hurricanes, sunflowers, and seashells. Branching is seen in the totally unrelated forms of frost

crystals, trees, and rivers. I immediately started dreaming about knitting these forms. I saw a kinship with my previous work and, at the same time, a new challenge. I chose themes from Ball's book to form the framework for my thoughts and experiments. The result is the six categories of patterns in nature that form the chapters in this book: Hexagons, Pentagons, Spirals, Phyllotaxis, Fractals, and Waves.

I know I have a reputation for loving patterns that look rather complicated. Truth be told, however, I am a bit lazy. I prefer to memorize cable and texture patterns as I knit rather than referencing a chart constantly. I like patterns and shaping to be logical, because that makes them easier to remember. I like things to look complicated, but have an underlying simplicity. Nature works the same way: The repetition of the simple rules of chemistry and physics form the seemingly complicated structures of flowers, clouds, coastlines, and snowflakes.

Some of the designs in this book are structurally similar to nature's example. The Bubble Pullover (page 50) is created by fitting together pentagonal (five-sided) pieces to form a three-dimensional bubble. The Cowl Pullover (page 79) and Nautilus Poncho (page 70) both form cone shapes, increasing in size from the inside out, just as shells do. Some designs, such as the Roundabout Leaf Tank (page 108), are merely inspired by the rules of nature. The Coastline Camisole and Skirt (page 141), the Triangle Scarf (page 146), and the Serpentine Coat (page 136) were all inspired by mathematical representations of patterns from nature.

In some cases, the structure of the natural phenomenon dictated the structure of the garment (the garments made from hexagonal and pentagonal pieces, for instance). In others, the pattern from nature becomes a surface decoration imposed on the grid of knitting, as is the case with the Branching Aran Guernsey (page 122), Vortex Street Pullover (page 152), and Honeycomb Henley (page 26). The patterning on all three of these is made with cables or twisted stitches. In all cases, working within the framework of six categories of patterns found in nature freed my mind to look at things differently and allowed me to rethink the structure of garment-making.

I've always felt I do my best work when given some limitations. I find the phase "do whatever you want" quite daunting. Limiting myself to patterns from nature provided me with a theme to hang my thoughts on in a cohesive manner. Each topic provided new limitations, which in turn allowed me to explore what could be achieved within these limitations. Of course, the designs in this book only begin to crack the surface. That's thrilling to me. I hope it is to you as well.

Chapter 1

HEXAGONS*

* hexagon: (n) a closed figure with six straight lines

From magnificent basalt columns formed from cooling lava to delicate, intricate skeletons of microscopic sea-dwelling diatoms, nature provides a rich diversity of hexagonal forms. Tortoise shells, wasp nests, insect eyes, and snowflakes all display a characteristic six-fold symmetry. The most graphic and familiar example of hexagons in nature is the honeycomb. Manufactured by bees as a storage area for food and a nursery for babies, a honeycomb is a marvel of engineering; it uses the least amount of material and labor to pack the greatest number of individual cells together.

The explanation of the hexagon's success in nature lies in the properties of bubbles. When forced into a single layer, as in a honeycomb, bubbles will always form hexagons. Liquids take on forms that require the least amount of surface area. This means that a single bubble is round, a sphere. Pack a few equal-sized bubbles side by side, and they will join sides and become hexagons. Other shapes are possible, like squares and triangles, but the 120° angles of hexagons are the most stable. Efficient and stable packing explains many (or perhaps all) of the hexagon forms occurring naturally in the world around us. The multiple spheres of insect eyes pack together to form hexagons. Radiolarians and diatoms—both types of plankton—produce a foam of hexagonal bubbles that hardens into their shells. Hexagons can be found outside of the animal realm, too. When a liquid is heated evenly, currents of hot liquid rising and cooler liquid falling form hexagon-shaped columns. Snowflakes are hexagonal because water crystals, like bubbles, pack together in six-fold symmetries.

This efficient packing is an ideal quality for knitting. Since hexagon motifs, like bubbles, fit together perfectly on a flat surface, it was easy for me to design knitwear with repeating hexagons. I invented a few twisted stitches and knit-purl patterns and used them as hexagonal "wallpaper" on traditional sweater constructions for the Asymmetrical Cardigan (page 12), the Honeycomb Henley (page 26), and the Hex Afghan (page 36). As an alternate approach to garment construction, hexagons are knitted from the outside in, then subsequent motifs are knitted on to make the curvaceous Basalt Tank (page 16), the Snapping Turtle Skirt (page 30), and the edging of the Hex Coat (page 22).

Asymmetrical Cardigan

When I first discovered them, Barbara Walker's knitting stitch dictionaries made my skin tingle. I memorized many of their pages. With each new stitch I tried, I learned more about the geometry and structure of lace, cables, and "simple" knit and purl patterns. I developed a vocabulary of stitches and techniques, and with them, I discovered I could "draw" with knitted stitches like one draws with ink on paper. Cables and twisted stitches form the lines and the patterned and plain stitches provide shadows and textures. Sometimes, it's not the stitch that is the hexagon, but the negative space created by it.

A more recent spine-tingling find is Archibald H. Christie's Pattern Design, a scholarly classic originally published in 1910. Christie wrote with an old-fashioned art historian's erudite seriousness that seems humorous today, but every time I crack the spine, a new aspect of it seems relevant to my current work. For example, Christie mentions how, historically, mimicry of one craft in another medium has been a powerful force in pattern design. Wallpaper patterns imitated tile designs. Carpet patterns were mimicked by silk weavers and tile painters. When I designed the stitch in this cardigan, I was imitating the woven pattern of caned chair seats. The interlacing horizontal and diagonal bands are interpreted in knitting by diagonal crossed stitches and horizontal garter ridges. The shape left in the middle? A hexagon.

SIZES
Petite (Small, Medium, Large, X-Large)
Shown in size Small

FINISHED MEASUREMENTS
36 (40, 44, 48, 52)"

YARN
Lang Cashmere Luxe (100% cashmere; 54 yards/25 grams): 20 (22, 25, 27, 29) balls #20 light blue

NEEDLES
One pair straight needles size US 9 (5.5 mm)
One pair straight needles size US 10 (6 mm)
Change needle size if necessary to obtain correct gauge.

NOTIONS
Stitch holder; split ring marker; three 1" buttons

GAUGE
18 sts and 25 rows = 4" (10 cm) in Twist Stitch Pattern using larger needles

NOTES

❭ Garment is worked in one piece, starting with Fronts, adding Sleeves and joining to Back.

❭ You may find it easier to work the Fronts at the same time with separate balls of yarn.

❭ When working shaping, if there are not enough sts to work RT or LT at beginning or end of row, work as k1.

LEFT FRONT

Using smaller needles, CO 33 (37, 41, 45, 49) sts; begin 2×2 Rib as follows: (WS) P1 (edge st, keep in St st), *k2, p2; repeat from * to end. Work even as established for 3", ending with a RS row. (WS) Change to larger needles, purl 1 row, increase 1 (1, 1, 3, 3) sts across row—34 (38, 42, 48, 52) sts. (RS) Change to Twist Stitch Pattern: K1 (edge st, keep in St st), work in Twist Stitch Pattern from Chart, beginning and ending where indicated for your size, to last st, k1 (edge st, keep in St st). Work even until piece measures 13" from the beginning, ending with a WS row.

Shape Sleeve: (RS) CO 2 sts at beginning of row every other row 12 times, 16 sts every other row twice, then 8 sts every other row once—98 (102, 106, 112, 116) sts. Work even until piece measures 21 (21½, 22, 22½, 23)" from the beginning, ending with a RS row.

Shape Front Neck: (WS) BO 4 sts at neck edge once, 2 sts twice, then decrease 1 st twice—88 (92, 96, 102, 106) sts remain. Work even until piece measures 23 (23½, 24, 24½, 25)" from the beginning, ending with a WS row.

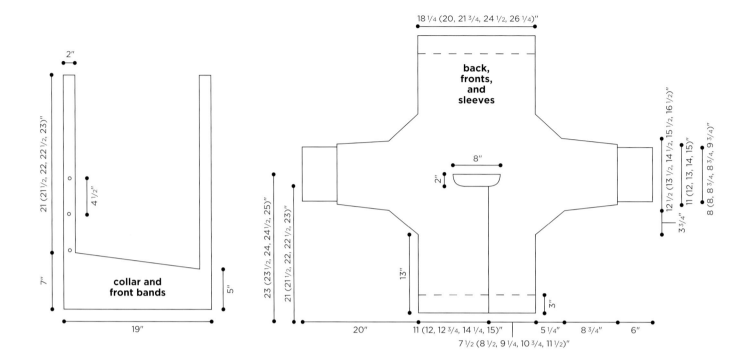

RIGHT FRONT

Using smaller needles, CO 51 (55, 59, 67, 71) sts; begin 2×2 Rib as follows: (WS) P2, *k2, p2; repeat from * to last st, p1 (edge st, keep in St st). Work even as established for 3″, ending with a RS row. (WS) Change to larger needles and purl 1 row, decrease 1 (1, 1, 3, 3) sts across row—50 (54, 58, 64, 68) sts remain. (RS) Change to Twist Stitch Pattern from Chart, beginning and ending where indicated for your size, and work as for Left Front to Sleeve shaping, ending with a RS row.

Shape Sleeve: (WS) CO 2 sts at beginning of row every other row 12 times, 16 sts every other row twice, then 8 sts every other row once—114 (118, 122, 128, 132) sts. Work even until piece measures 21 (21½, 22, 22½, 23)″ from the beginning, ending with a WS row.

Shape Front Neck: (RS) BO 18 sts at neck edge once, 4 sts twice, 2 sts twice, then decrease 1 st twice—86 (90, 94, 100, 104) sts remain. Work even until piece measures same as for Left Front, ending with the same row. Break yarn. Place sts on holder.

BACK

(RS) Work across 88 (92, 96, 102, 106) Left Front sts, CO 36 sts for neck, work across 86 (90, 94, 100, 104) Right Front sts from holder—210 (218, 226, 238, 246) sts. Work even for 5 (5½, 6, 6½)″, ending with a WS row.

Shape Sleeve: (RS) BO 8 sts at beginning of next 2 rows, 16 sts at beginning of next 4 rows, then 2 sts at beginning of next 24 rows—82 (90, 98, 110, 118) sts remain. Work even for 13″, ending with a RS row. (WS) Change to smaller needles, purl 1 row. Change to 2×2 Rib as follows: K2, *p2, k2; repeat from * to end. Work even for 3″. BO all sts.

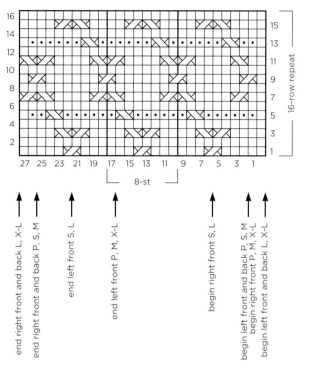

KEY

▢ Knit on RS, purl on WS.

▣ Purl on RS, knit on WS.

◩ K2tog, but do not drop sts from left-hand needle, insert right-hand needle between 2 sts just worked and knit first st again, slip both sts from left-hand needle together.

◪ Knit into back of second st, then knit first and second sts together through back loops, slip both sts from left-hand needle together.

FINISHING

Cuffs: Using smaller needles, pick up and knit 38 (38, 42, 42, 46) sts along bottom of Sleeve. (WS) Begin 2×2 Rib as follows: P2, *k2, p2, repeat from * to end. Work even for 6″. BO all sts. Sew side and Sleeve seams.

Bands and Collar: Using smaller needles, CO 90 sts; begin Rib as follows: (WS) [P1, k1] 4 times, *p2, k2; repeat from * to last 10 sts, p2, [k1, p1] 4 times. Work even for 5″. Next row (RS), work 9 sts, place on holder for left Front Band, BO 12 sts in pattern, work to end. Work 1 row even. BO 12 sts in pattern at beginning of row every other row 5 times—9 sts remain; place row marker. *Right Front Band:* Work even for 2 rows. *Buttonhole Row:* (RS) Work 4 sts, yo, k2tog, work to end. *Work even for 4½″, ending with a WS row. Work Buttonhole Row. Repeat from * once. Work even until Band measures 21 (21½, 22, 22½, 23)″ from marker when slightly stretched. BO all sts. *Left Front Band:* Join yarn and work across 9 sts from holder, pm, work even until Band measures 21 (21½, 22, 22½, 23)″ from marker when slightly stretched. BO all sts. Sew Collar to neck and sew Bands to Front edges. Sew buttons opposite buttonholes.

Basalt Tank

Basalt is rock formed by molten lava. As the lava is cooling, the cooler rock falls to the bottom of the liquid while the warmer rock rises to the top. The currents in the lava form tall hexagonal columns, and later, when the rock solidifies, it is frozen in these shapes, one column fitted closely to the next. Think of it as the vertical version of the hexagons in this tank.

The process of engineering this tank was an exercise in paring a shape down to its mathematical core—or an exercise in laziness. Rather than carving out the perfectly rounded armhole and debating the depth of the modest yet sexy neckline, I let the hexagonal structure determine all shaping. The armholes are shaped by omitting one wedge (one-sixth) of the hexagon pattern. An elaborately cascading hemline results from letting the edges of each hexagonal motif shape the finished edge. Even the neck and shoulder banding is plucked straight from the hexagon pattern and shaping. Turns out, the long-sided version is, without a doubt, the most flattering hand-knit sweater I have ever had on my rounded five-foot frame. For the wasp-waisted and young, a second version is made by omitting the two side hexagons.

SIZES

To fit Adult <Teen>
X-Small (Small, Medium, Large, X-Large)
Shown in size Small <X-Small>

FINISHED MEASUREMENTS

33 (36, 39, 42, 45)" chest

YARN

Rowan Wool Cotton (50% merino wool/50% cotton; 123 yards/50 grams): 6 (7, 7, 8, 8) balls #943 flower <4 (5, 5, 6, 6) balls #956 coffee rich>

NEEDLES

One pair straight needles size US 4 (3.5 mm)
Change needle size if necessary to obtain correct gauge.

NOTIONS

Stitch markers

GAUGE

22 sts and 30 rows = 4" (10 cm) in Stockinette st (St st)

NOTES

❩ Adult and Teen sizes are worked the same, with the exception that Teen sizes do not work Hexagons 2 and 3. Where Adult sizes pick up and knit sts from Hexagons 2 and 3, Teen sizes (shown in <>) CO the same number of sts as are picked up. Where there is only one set of numbers, it applies to both Adult and Teen sizes.

❩ Each Hexagon is worked in segments, between markers. Full Hexagons have six segments; the first and sixth segment are seamed together to complete the Hexagon. The ⅚ and ½ Hexagons have 5 and 3 segments respectively. See Schematic for assembly.

❩ CO using a tail method. For each Hexagon where you will pick up sts from an existing piece, make sure that your tail is long enough to complete the pick up's and CO's around the entire edge. When you pick up sts following a CO, pick up the first st with the tail end and the next st with the ball end; alternate this way across the entire pick-up section, so that the two ends will be in place for the next CO.

❩ Decrease Row: K1, *k2tog, knit to 2 sts before marker, ssk; repeat from * to last st, k1.

FULL HEXAGON 1

CO 188 (200, 212, 224, 236) sts. Place marker (pm) after first st, and after every 31 (33, 35, 37, 39) sts thereafter.

Establish Pattern:

Rows 1, 3 and 5 (WS): P1, knit to last st, p1.

Row 2: Work Decrease Row—29 (31, 33, 35, 37) sts remain between markers.

Rows 4, 8, 12, 16 and 22: Knit.

Rows 6, 10, 14, 18 and 20: Repeat Row 2—19 (21, 23, 25, 27) sts remain between markers after Row 20.

Row 7: P1, *p1, yo, p2tog; repeat from * to last st, p1.

Rows 9, 11 and 13: P1, knit to last st, p1.

Rows 15, 17, 19, 21 and 23: Purl.

Row 24: Repeat Row 2—17 (19, 21, 23, 25) sts remain between markers.

Sizes S (M, L, X-L) only:

Rows 25 and 27: Purl.

Row 26: Repeat Row 2—17 (19, 21, 23) sts remain between markers.

Row 28: Knit.

Sizes M (L, X-L) only:

Row 29: Purl.

Row 30: Repeat Row 2—17 (19, 21) sts remain between markers.

Sizes L (X-L) only:

Rows 31 and 33: Purl.

Row 32: Repeat Row 2—17 (19) sts remain between markers.

Row 34: Knit.

Size X-L only:

Rows 35 and 37: Purl.

Row 36: Repeat Row 2—17 sts remain between markers.

Row 38: Knit.

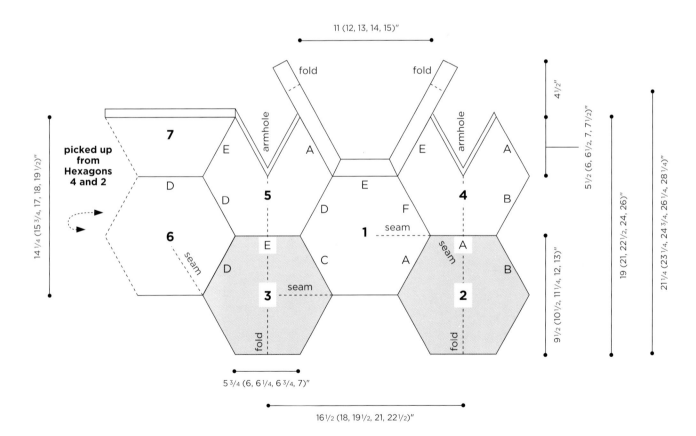

NOTE: Hexagons 2 and 3 (shown in gray) are not worked for Teen sizes.

All Sizes: 17 sts remain between markers—104 sts total.

Inside Section

Rows 1, 3, 5, 9, 11, 13, 15 and 17 (WS): P1, knit to last st, p1.

Row 2: Work Decrease Row—15 sts remain between markers.

Rows 4, 6, 10, 12, 14, and 16: Repeat Row 2—3 sts remain between markers after Row 16.

Row 7: P1, *p1, yo, p2tog; repeat from * to last st, p1.

Row 8: Knit.

Row 18: K1, *slip 2 sts together as if to k2tog, k1, psso, repeat from * to last st, k1—8 sts remain.

Break yarn, thread through remaining sts and pull tight; sew first and sixth segments together along shaped edges.

Adults Only
FULL HEXAGON 2

CO 156 (166, 176, 186, 196) sts, pick up and knit 32 (34, 36, 38, 40) sts along side A of Hexagon 1—188 (200, 212, 224, 236) sts. Work as for Hexagon 1.

Adults Only
FULL HEXAGON 3

CO 156 (166, 176, 186, 196) sts, pick up and knit 32 (34, 36, 38, 40) sts along side C of Hexagon 1—188 (200, 212, 224, 236) sts. Work as for Hexagon 1.

All Sizes
⁵/₆ HEXAGON 4

CO 63 (67, 71, 75, 79) sts, pick up and knit 31 (33, 35, 37, 39) sts along side A of Hexagon 2 <CO 31 (33, 35, 37, 39) sts>, pick up and knit 31 (33, 35, 37, 39) sts along side F of Hexagon 1, CO 32 (34, 36, 38, 40) sts—157 (167, 177, 187, 197) sts. Work as for Hexagon 1; you will have completed 5 segments—7 sts remain. Break yarn, thread through remaining sts and pull tight. Do not sew segments together.

⁵/₆ HEXAGON 5

CO 32 (34, 36, 38, 40) sts, pick up and knit 31 (33, 35, 37, 39) sts along side D of Hexagon 1, and 31 (33, 35, 37, 39) sts along side E of Hexagon 3 <CO 31, 33, 35, 37, 39) sts>, CO 32 (34, 36, 38, 40) sts—157 (167, 177, 187, 197) sts. Work as for Hexagon 4.

FULL HEXAGON 6

CO 32 (34, 36, 38, 40) sts, pick up and knit 31 (33, 35, 37, 39) sts along side B of Hexagon 2 <CO 31 (33, 35, 37, 39) sts>, pick up and knit 31 (33, 35, 37, 39) sts along side B of Hexagon 4, CO 31 (33, 35, 37, 39) sts, pick up and knit 31 (33, 35, 37, 39) sts along side D of Hexagon 5, and 31 (33, 35, 37, 39) sts along side D of Hexagon 3 <CO 31 (33, 35, 37, 39) sts>—188 (200, 212, 224, 236) sts. Work as for Hexagon 1.

¹/₂ HEXAGON 7

Pick up and knit 32 (34, 36, 38, 40) sts along side E of Hexagon 5, 31 (33, 35, 37, 39) sts along side D of Hexagon 6, and 32 (34, 36, 38, 40) sts along side A of Hexagon 4—95 (101, 107, 113, 119) sts. Work as for Hexagon 1; you will have completed 3 segments—5 sts remain. Break yarn, thread through remaining sts and pull tight. Do not sew segments together.

Sew Hexagons 7 and 6 to 4 and 2 as indicated on diagram.

FINISHING

Armhole Edges: Pick up and knit 31 (33, 35, 37, 39) sts from top of ⅚ Hexagon to bottom of armhole edge, pm, pick up and knit 31 (33, 35, 37, 39) sts to end of armhole—62 (66, 70, 74, 78) sts. Next 2 rows: Knit to 2 sts before marker, ssk, slip marker (sm), k2tog, knit to end—58 (62, 66, 70, 74) sts remain. BO all sts knitwise. *Back Neck:* Pick up and knit 62 (66, 70, 74, 78) sts along top of Back. Knit 4 rows. BO all sts knitwise. *Front Neck and Straps:* CO 26 sts, pick up and knit 31 (33, 35, 37, 39) sts along left Front neck edge, pm, pick up and knit 31 (33, 35, 37, 39) sts along bottom neck edge, pm, pick up and knit 31 (33, 35, 37) sts along right Front neck edge, CO 26 sts—145 (151, 157, 163, 169) sts. Work Neckband and Straps as follows:

Rows 1, 3 and 5 (WS): P1, knit to last st, p1.

Rows 2, 6 and 10: [Knit to 2 sts before marker, ssk, sm, k2tog] twice, knit to end —133 (139, 145, 151, 157) sts remain after Row 10.

Rows 4, 8 and 12: Knit.

Row 7: P1, *p1, p2tog, yo; repeat from * to last st, end p1.

Rows 9 and 11: P1, knit to last st, p1.

BO all sts knitwise. Sew ends of Straps to Back neck.

Hex Coat

While hexagons fit together perfectly in a flat plane, their six-sided geometry allows them to fit together in myriad other ways. Depending upon which edges you choose to join, they can form straight lines, curves, and waves. In this coat, the hexagons form their signature flat pattern in the background, then are joined end to end, like a string of pearls, to trim the neckline and create a long, flattering visual line.

I've been designing professionally for twenty years now, and in that time, I've designed quite a few sweaters—more than 1,200, by my loose calculations. And while they all tend to look great on models, I've come to realize that many don't look right on me. I'm five feet tall and curvy, and a goal of mine is to design more sweaters that I, myself, can wear. Long coats like this one are favorites in my wardrobe; I think it's the long, simple line. Narrow, set-in sleeves give a clean shape without adding extra bulk. The hexagon chain around the neckline—which catches the eye and draws it down along the line—proves to be very slimming as well.

NOTES

▶ *Stitch Patterns:* see right.

▶ The Fronts must have a specific number of indentations so the Hexagon Trim will fit. Therefore, it is important to work at least one Front before you work the Back, to ensure that your row gauge is correct. If the row gauge is incorrect, it will affect the length of the garment to the underarm, and you will need to adjust the length of the Back to the underarm to match the Front.

▶ CO using a tail method. For each Hexagon where you will pick up sts from an existing piece, make sure that your tail is long enough to complete the CO's and pick up's around the entire edge. When you pick up sts following a CO, pick up the first st with the tail end and the next st with the ball end; alternate this way across the entire pick-up section.

▶ *Left Decrease Row:* (RS) Work to last 4 sts, k2tog, k2.
▶ *Left Increase Row:* (RS) Work to last 3 sts, m1, k3.
▶ *Right Decrease Row:* (RS) K2, ssk, work to end.
▶ *Right Increase Row:* (RS) K3, m1, work to end.

LEFT FRONT

Using smallest (size US 6) needles, CO 34 (40, 44, 50, 54) sts.

Establish Pattern: (RS) Work in 1×1 Rib to last 3 sts, k3. Next row and all WS rows: P3, work as established to end.

Shape Center Edge: (RS) Continuing in 1×1 Rib as established, work Left Decrease Row every other row 5 times—29 (35, 39, 45, 49) sts remain. (WS) Change to largest (size US 8) needles and Moss St. Work even for 3 rows. (RS) Continuing in Moss St as established, work Left Increase Row every other row 5 times—34 (40, 44, 50, 54) sts. (WS) Work even for 3 rows. *(RS) Work Left Decrease Row every other row 5 times—29 (35, 39, 45, 49) sts remain. (WS) Work even for 3 rows. (RS) Work Left Increase Row every other row 5 times—34 (40, 44, 50, 54) sts. (WS) Work even for 3 rows.* (RS) Repeat between * 6 (6, 6, 5, 5) times [8 (8, 8, 7, 7) complete indentations worked from the beginning]. Piece should measure approximately 31 (31, 31, 27¼, 27¼)" from the beginning. (RS) Continuing Center Edge shaping, work 8 (4, 0, 16, 20) more rows.

SIZES
Petite (Small, Medium, Large, X-Large)
Shown in size Petite

FINISHED MEASUREMENTS
41½ (46, 51, 56½, 60)" chest, including Hexagon Trim

YARN
Reynolds Yarns Lite Lopi (100% Icelandic wool; 109 yards/50 grams): 16 (18, 20, 21, 23) skeins. Shown in #421 celery heather

NEEDLES
One pair straight needles size US 6 (4 mm)

One pair straight needles size US 8 (5 mm)

One set of four 6" double-pointed needles (dpn) size 7 (4.5 mm) for hexagon trim

Change needle size if necessary to obtain correct gauge.

NOTIONS
Stitch markers

GAUGE
17 sts and 25 rows = 4" (10 cm) in Moss St using largest (size US 8) needles

STITCH PATTERNS
1×1 Rib:
(multiple of 2 sts; 1-row repeat)
All Rows: *K1, p1; repeat from * to end.

Moss Stitch:
(multiple of 2 sts; 4-row repeat)
Row 1 (RS): *P1, k1; repeat from * to end.
Row 2: *P1, k1; repeat from * to end.
Rows 3 and 4: *K1, p1; repeat from * to end.
Repeat Rows 1–4 for Moss Stitch.

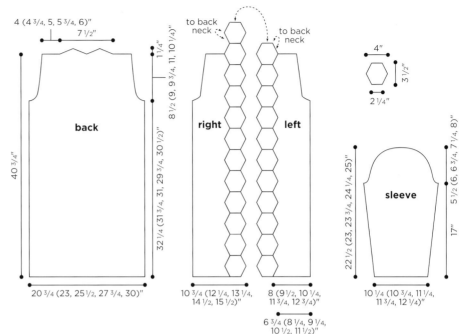

Shape Armhole: (RS) BO 4 sts at armhole edge 1 (1, 1, 2, 3) times, 3 sts 1 (2, 3, 3, 2) times, 2 sts 1 (1, 1, 1, 2) times, then decrease 1 st at armhole edge 3 (3, 3, 2, 2) times. When 11th set of Center Edge decreases is finished (do not work corresponding increases), BO remaining 17 (20, 21, 24, 25) sts.

RIGHT FRONT

Work as for Left Front, reversing patterns and shaping, and working Right Decrease Row and Right Increase Row instead of Left Decrease Row and Left Increase Row.

BACK

Using smallest (size US 6) needles, CO 88 (98, 108, 118, 128) sts; begin 1×1 Rib. Work even for 2″, ending with a WS row. (RS) Change to largest (size US 8) needles and Moss St. Work even until piece measures same as for Left Front to armhole shaping, ending with a WS row.

Shape Armholes: (RS) BO 4 sts at beginning of next 2 (2, 2, 4, 6) rows, 3 sts at beginning of next 2 (4, 6, 6, 4) rows, 2 sts at beginning of next 2 (2, 2, 2, 4) rows, then dec 1 st each side every other row 6 (6, 6, 4, 4) times—64 (68, 72, 76, 80) sts remain. Work even until piece measures same as for Left Front to shoulder, ending with a WS row. (RS) BO 17 (19, 21, 23, 25) sts at beginning of next 2 rows—32 sts remain. Work 1 row even.

Shape Neck: Mark center. (RS) BO 2 sts, work to marker; join a second ball of yarn, BO 2 sts and work to end. Working BOTH SIDES AT SAME TIME, BO 2 sts at each neck and shoulder edge until no sts remain.

SLEEVES (make 2)

Using smallest (size US 6) needles, CO 44 (46, 48, 50, 52) sts; begin 1×1 Rib. Work even for 2″, ending with a WS row. (RS) Change to largest (size US 8) needles and Moss St. Work even for 2 rows.

Shape Sleeve: (RS) Increase 1 st each side every 12 (10, 8, 8, 8) rows 8 (9, 10, 11, 12) times as follows: K1, m1, work to last st, m1, k1—60 (64, 68, 72, 76) sts. Work even until piece measures 17″ from the beginning, ending with a WS row.

Shape Cap: (RS) BO 3 sts at beginning of next 2 rows, 2 sts at beginning of next 2 rows, then dec 1 st each side every other row 3 times, every 4 rows 3 (4, 5, 6, 7) times, then every other row 4 times as follows: Ssk, work to last 2 sts, k2tog. BO 2 sts at beginning of next 2 rows, then 3 sts at beginning of next 2 rows—20 (22, 24, 26, 28) sts remain. BO all sts.

FINISHING

Sew shoulder seams. Set in Sleeves. Sew side and Sleeve seams.

HEXAGON TRIM

First Hexagon: Using dpn, CO 40 sts; divide sts evenly on 2 needles. Using a third needle, beginning at bottom of Right Front, pick up and knit 20 sts along shaping edges of one indentation (10 sts each slope)—60 sts. Join for working in the rnd, being careful not to twist sts; place marker (pm) after every 10 sts. Purl one rnd. Decrease Rnd: *K2tog, knit to 2 sts before marker, ssk; repeat from * around—48 sts remain. Purl 1 rnd. Knit 1 rnd. Purl 1 rnd. Repeat Decrease Rnd—36 sts remain. Purl 1 rnd. [Knit 2 rnds, repeat Decrease Rnd] twice—12 sts remain. Thread yarn through remaining loops, pull tight and fasten off.

Remaining Hexagons: Using dpn, CO 30 sts. Divide sts evenly on 2 needles. Using a third needle, pick up and knit 20 sts in one Front indentation (10 sts each slope), pick up 10 sts along edge of preceding Hexagon—60 sts. Join for working in the rnd, being careful not to twist sts; pm after every 10 sts. Work as for first Hexagon. *Note: The last Hexagon to be worked at the top of Right Front will pick up 10 sts along the last half indentation on the Front and 10 sts along the first slope of Back neck shaping. The following Hexagon will pick up 20 sts along the center Back neck indentation. The final Back Hexagon will pick up 10 sts along the final slope of Back neck shaping and 10 sts along the half indentation at the top of the Left Front.*

Honeycomb Henley

SIZES
X-Small (Small, Medium, Large, X-Large)
Shown in size Small

FINISHED MEASUREMENTS
36 ½ (40 ½, 44 ½, 48 ½, 52 ½)" chest

YARN
Goddess Yarns Emmanuella (100% merino wool; 90 yards/50 grams): 16 (18, 20, 22, 24) balls #8320 taupe

NEEDLES
One pair straight needles size US 6 (3.5 mm)

One pair straight needles size US 7 (4.5 mm)

Change needle size if necessary to obtain correct gauge.

NOTIONS
Stitch markers

GAUGE
24 sts and 28 rows = 4" (10 cm) in Honeycomb Pattern using larger needles

STITCH PATTERNS
2×2 Rib:
(multiple of 4 sts + 2; 2-row repeat)
Row 1 (RS): K2, *p2, k2; repeat from * to end.
Row 2: P2, *k2, p2; repeat from * to end.
Repeat Rows 1 and 2 for 2×2 Rib.

Honeycomb Pattern:
(multiple of 6 sts + 2; 16-row repeat)
Rows 1, 3, 7, 9, 11 and 15 (WS): *P2, k1; repeat from * to last 2 sts, p2.
Rows 2, 8 and 10: *K2, p1; repeat from * to last 2 sts, k2.
Row 4: K1, *k1, RT, LT, k1; repeat from * to last st, k1.
Row 6: K1, *RT, k2, LT; repeat from * to last st, k1.
Rows 5 and 13: Purl.
Row 12: K1, *LT, k2, RT; repeat from * to last st, k1.
Row 14: K1, *k1, LT, RT, k1; repeat from * to last st, k1.
Row 16: *K2, p1; repeat from * to last 2 sts, k2.
Repeat rows 1–16 for Honeycomb Pattern.

This henley-style sweater features a simple hexagonal organization of twisted stitches, one of my favorite design tools. Just like cells in a honeycomb, these twisted-stitch hexagons fit together perfectly to create a flat, uninterrupted pattern of six-sided shapes.

My infatuation with twisted stitches began years ago, at a presentation in which Vogue Knitting unveiled to designers the colors and themes for an upcoming issue. I left with my head full of images and textures and details. One slide in particular was a huge turning point for me. It showed an oversized "cable" composed of twisted stitches that formed a pattern on the surface of the knitting. I experimented for hours, days, and eventually years. I had discovered a new love.

Twenty years later, twisted stitches still inspire me, but I've brought them into a new realm—that of geometric shapes. Here, I've manipulated them to form the hexagonal "wallpaper" that forms the fabric of this sweater.

NOTES
❱ *Stitch Patterns:* see left.

❱ *LT:* Knit into back of second st, then knit first and second sts together through back loops, slip both sts from left-hand needle together.

❱ *RT:* K2tog, but do not drop sts from left-hand needle, insert right-hand needle between 2 sts just worked and knit the first st again, drop both sts from left-hand needle together.

BACK
Using smaller needles, CO 110 (122, 134, 146, 158) sts; begin 2×2 Rib. Work even for 5", ending with a RS row. (WS) Change to larger needles and Honeycomb Pattern from Chart. Work even until piece measures 15" from the beginning, ending with a WS row.

Shape Armholes:

Size X-L only:

BO 6 sts at beginning of next 2 rows.

All sizes:

BO 4 sts at beginning of next 2 (2, 2, 4, 2) rows, 3 sts at beginning of next 2 (4, 4, 4, 6) rows, 2 sts at beginning of next 4 (4, 6, 6, 4) rows, then decrease 1 st each side every other row 1 (1, 2, 1, 1) times—86 (92, 98, 104, 110) sts remain. Work even until armhole measures 7 ½ (8, 8 ½, 9, 9 ½)" from the beginning of shaping, ending with a WS row.

Shape Neck and Shoulders: (RS) Work 35 (37, 38, 40, 42) sts; join a second ball of yarn and BO center 16 (18, 22, 24, 26) sts, work to end. Working BOTH SIDES AT SAME TIME, BO 4 sts at each neck edge 3 times, and AT THE SAME TIME, beginning on next RS row, BO 8 (8, 9, 9, 10) sts at beginning of next 4 rows, then 7 (9, 8, 10, 10) sts at beginning of next 2 rows.

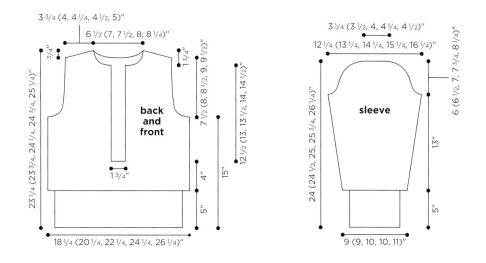

Measurements (back and front):

3 3/4 (4, 4 1/4, 4 1/2, 5)"

6 1/2 (7, 7 1/2, 8, 8 1/4)"

3/4"

1 3/4"

23 1/4 (23 3/4, 24 1/4, 24 3/4, 25 1/4)"

7 1/2 (8, 8 1/2, 9, 9 1/2)"

12 1/2 (13, 13 1/2, 14, 14 1/2)"

15"

4"

5"

1 3/4"

18 1/4 (20 1/4, 22 1/4, 24 1/4, 26 1/4)"

Measurements (sleeve):

3 1/4 (3 1/2, 4, 4 1/4, 4 1/2)"

12 1/4 (13 1/4, 14 1/4, 15 1/4, 16 1/4)"

6 (6 1/2, 7, 7 3/4, 8 1/4)"

24 (24 1/2, 25, 25 3/4, 26 1/4)"

13"

5"

9 (9, 10, 10, 11)"

FRONT

Work as for Back until piece measures 9″ from the beginning, ending with a WS row.

Shape Placket: (RS) Continuing in Honeycomb Pattern, work 50 (56, 62, 68, 74) sts; join a second ball of yarn and BO center 10 sts, work to end. Work even until piece measures 15″ from the beginning, ending with a WS row. (RS) Shape armholes as for Back—38 (41, 44, 47, 50) sts remain each side. Work even until Placket opening measures 12 1/2 (13, 13 1/2, 14, 14 1/2)″ from the beginning, ending with a WS row.

Shape Neck: (RS) BO 6 sts at each neck edge once, 4 sts 1 (1, 1, 2, 2) times, 3 sts 1 (1, 2, 1, 1) times, 2 sts once, then decrease 1 st 0 (1, 0, 0, 1) time and AT THE SAME TIME, when piece measures same as Back to shoulder, shape shoulders as for Back.

SLEEVES (make 2)

Using smaller needles, CO 54 (54, 60, 60, 66) sts; begin 2×2 Rib. Work even for 5″, ending with a RS row. (WS) Change to larger needles and Honeycomb Pattern. Work even for 1″, ending with a WS row.

Shape Sleeve: (RS) Continuing in Honeycomb Pattern, increase 1 st each side this row, then every 8 (6, 6, 4, 4) rows 9 (12, 12, 15, 15) times as follows: K1, m1, work to last st, m1, k1—74 (80, 86, 92, 98) sts. Work even until piece measures 18″ from the beginning, ending with a WS row.

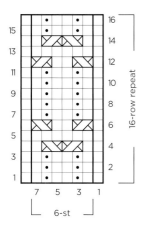

KEY

☐   Knit on RS, purl on WS.

⊡   Purl on RS, knit on WS.

▨   **RT:** K2tog, but do not drop sts from left-hand needle, insert right-hand needle between 2 sts just worked and knit the first st again, slip both sts from left-hand needle together.

▨   **LT:** Knit into back of second st, then knit first and second sts together through back loops, slip both sts from left-hand needle together.

Shape Cap: (RS) BO 4 sts at beginning of next 2 rows, 3 sts at beginning of next 2 rows, 2 sts at beginning of next 2 rows. Decrease 1 st each side this row, every other row 1 (2, 3, 4, 5) times, every 4 rows 6 times, then every other row 1 (2, 3, 4, 5) times as follows: Ssk, work to last 2 sts, k2tog—36 (40, 44, 48, 52) sts remain. BO 2 sts at beginning of next 2 rows, 3 sts at beginning of next 2 rows, then 4 sts at beginning of next 2 rows—20 (22, 24, 26, 28) sts remain. BO remaining sts.

FINISHING

Block all pieces to measurements. Sew shoulder seams. Set in Sleeves. Sew side and Sleeve seams.

Neckband: Using smaller needles, beginning at right neck edge, pick up and knit 80 (84, 92, 96, 100) sts around neck shaping; begin 2×2 Rib as follows: (WS): P1, *p2, k2; repeat from * to last 3 sts, p3. Continue as established, keeping first and last st in St st. Work even for 2½". BO all sts in pattern.

Plackets: Using smaller needles, pick up and knit 72 (84, 92, 96, 100) sts along left Front Placket opening and Neckband; begin 2×2 Rib as for Neckband, keeping first and last st in St st. Work even for 2". BO all sts in pattern. Sew bottom ends of Placket to Body, placing right Placket over left Placket.

Snapping Turtle Skirt

When I was fourteen, my mother bought me Elizabeth Zimmermann's Knitting Without Tears *because I was, and still am, such a crier when it comes to my knitting. I learned many useful lessons from the chatty pages. When Zimmermann discovered techniques that probably weren't new, just unknown to her, she claimed she "unvented" them. The shaping of this skirt seemed like a knitting epiphany to me, but I have the feeling I've unvented it, too, and that nature did it first. To increase the circumference at the bottom edge, working from the top down, I made each hexagon an increment larger than the one above it. The result is a gentle A-line silhouette with no evident signs of shaping. If you look at a turtle shell, you'll see that nature has bent and sized its hexagon "scales" to cover the dome of the shell in a very similar manner.*

Another trick, this time one I picked up from Seventh Avenue ready-to-wear designers, was useful in making this skirt. When evaluating a knitted stitch pattern, they'll flip a swatch over to examine the wrong side, because it's often more intriguing than the intended right side. In this case, the raised seams on the "wrong" side, made by picking up stitches on each edge, highlighted the perimeters of the hexagons, lending visual clarity. I like the color mixing and the texture of the reverse Stockinette stitch as well.

SIZES

To fit hip 32 (34, 36, 38, 40, 42, 44, 46, 48)"
Shown in size 34

FINISHED MEASUREMENTS

Hip 32¾ (35, 37¼, 39½, 41½, 43¾, 46, 48¼, 50¼)"
Length 21½ (23, 24¼, 25¾, 27, 28½, 29¾, 31¼, 32½)"

YARN

Berroco Suede (100% nylon; 120 yards/50 grams): 8 (8, 10, 11, 12, 13, 14, 15, 16) balls #3745, calamity Jane

NEEDLES

One set of four double-pointed needles (dpn) size US 8 (5 mm)
One 24" (60 cm) or 29" (74 cm) circular (circ) needle size US 8 (5 mm)
Change needle size if necessary to obtain correct gauge.

NOTIONS

Stitch markers (6); one skirt zipper 7 (7, 8, 8, 9, 9, 10, 10)"; one hook and eye closure (optional)

GAUGE

19 sts and 28 rows = 4" (10 cm) in Stockinette stitch (St st)

NOTES

▶ Follow assembly diagram for proper order to work and assemble Triangles and Hexagons.

▶ Once the skirt is finished, you will turn it inside out so that the Rev St st side will become the right side of the skirt. However, all pieces will be worked on the St st side, which, for the purposes of the instructions, will be considered the RS. All of the pieces are picked up on the RS, which leaves all the pick-up ridges facing out once the skirt is finished, to further define the hexagons.

▶ CO using a tail method. For each Hexagon where you will pick up sts from an existing piece, make sure that your tail is long enough to complete the CO's and pick up's around the entire edge. When you pick up sts following a CO, pick up the first st with the tail end and the next st with the ball end; alternate this way across the entire pick-up section.

▶ *Decrease Row (RS):* K1, k2tog, knit to last 3 sts, ssk, k1.

▶ *Double Decrease Row (RS):* K1, k3tog, knit to last 4 sts, sssk, k1.

▶ *Decrease Rnd:* [K2tog, knit to 2 sts before next marker, ssk] 6 times.

SKIRT

(made of 5 Waist Triangles, 2 Edge Triangles, and 24 Hexagons)

WAIST TRIANGLES (make 5)

CO 22 (24, 26, 27, 29, 30, 32, 33, 35) sts; purl 1 (WS) row and all WS rows.

Shape Triangle: (RS) Work Double Decrease Row every other row 3 (4, 5, 4, 5, 6, 6, 6, 7) times. Work Decrease Row every other row 3 (2, 1, 3, 2, 1, 2, 2, 1) times—4 (4, 4, 5, 5, 4, 4, 5, 5) sts remain. Work 1 row even. Next row (RS), K2tog, k0 (0, 0, 1, 1, 0, 0, 1, 1) st, ssk—2 (2, 2, 3, 3, 2, 2, 3, 3) sts remain. BO all sts.

RIGHT ZIPPER EDGE TRIANGLE

CO 12 (13, 14, 14, 15, 16, 17, 17, 18) sts; purl next (WS) row and all WS rows.

Shape Triangle: (RS) Decrease 2 sts every other row 3 (4, 5, 4, 5, 6, 6, 6, 7) times as follows: K1, k3tog, knit to end. Decrease 1 st every other row 4 (3, 2, 4, 3, 2, 3, 3, 2) times as follows: K1, k2tog, knit to end—2 sts remain. BO all sts.

LEFT ZIPPER EDGE TRIANGLE

CO 12 (13, 14, 14, 15, 16, 17, 17, 18) sts; purl next (WS) row and all WS rows.

Shape Triangle: (RS) Decrease 2 sts every other row 3 (4, 5, 4, 5, 6, 6, 6, 7) times as follows: K1, k3tog, knit to end. Decrease 1 st every other row 4 (3, 2, 4, 3, 2, 3, 3, 2) times as follows: K1, k2tog, knit to end—2 sts remain. BO all sts.

ROW 1 HEXAGONS

Using dpn, CO 30 (32, 34, 36, 38, 40, 42, 44, 46) sts each on Needles 1 and 2; using Needle 3, with RS of Right Zipper Edge Triangle and one Waist Triangle facing, pick up and knit 15 (16, 17, 18, 19, 20, 21, 22, 23) sts each along right-hand shaping edge of Waist Triangle and shaping edge of Right Zipper Edge Triangle—90 (96, 102, 108, 114, 120, 126, 132, 138) sts. Join for working in the rnd, being careful not to twist sts; place marker (pm) after every 15 (16, 17, 18, 19, 20, 21, 22, 23) sts—this marks the 6 sides of the Hexagon.

Shape Hexagon: Begin St st, *work one Decrease Rnd. Work two rnds even; repeat from * until 3 (2, 3, 2, 3, 2, 3, 2, 3) sts remain between markers—18 (12, 18, 12, 18, 12, 18, 12, 18) sts total. Work 2 (1, 2, 1, 2, 1, 2, 1, 2) rnds even. Next rnd, *k2tog; rep from * around—9 (6, 9, 6, 9, 6, 9, 6, 9) sts remain. Break yarn, thread through remaining sts, pull tight and fasten off.

Work 5 more Hexagons as follows: CO 15 (16, 17, 18, 19, 20, 21, 22, 23, 24) sts for each of the 3 unattached sides and pick up and knit 15 (16, 17, 18, 19, 20, 21, 22, 23, 24) sts each along shaping edges of Waist Triangles and left-hand edge of preceding Hexagon, dividing sts evenly among needles so that there are 2 full sides per needle—90 (96, 102, 108, 114, 120, 126, 132, 138) sts. Complete as for first Hexagon.

ROW 2 HEXAGONS

Using dpn, CO 30 (32, 34, 36, 38, 40, 42, 44, 46) sts each on Needles 1 and 2; using Needle 3, CO 15 (16, 17, 18, 19, 20, 21, 22, 23, 24) sts, pick up and knit 15 (16, 17, 18, 19, 20, 21, 22, 23, 24) sts along right-hand bottom edge of first Hexagon in Row 1—90 (96, 102, 108, 114, 120, 126, 132, 138) sts. Join for working in the rnd, being careful not to twist sts; pm after every 15 (16, 17, 18, 19, 20, 21, 22, 23) sts—this marks the 6 sides of the Hexagon. Shape as for Row 1 Hexagon.

Work 5 more Hexagons as follows: CO 15 (16, 17, 18, 19, 20, 21, 22, 23, 24) sts for each of the 3 unattached sides and pick up and knit 15 (16, 17, 18, 19, 20, 21, 22, 23, 24) sts each along bottom edges of Hexagon in Row 1 and left-hand edge of preceding Hexagon, dividing sts evenly among needles so that there are 2 full sides per needle—90 (96, 102, 108, 114, 120, 126, 132, 138). Complete as for first Hexagon in Row 2.

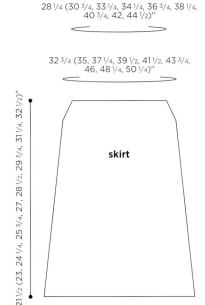

28 1/4 (30 3/4, 33 1/4, 34 1/4, 36 3/4, 38 1/4, 40 3/4, 42, 44 1/2)"

32 3/4 (35, 37 1/4, 39 1/2, 41 1/2, 43 3/4, 46, 48 1/4, 50 1/4)"

skirt

21 1/2 (23, 24 1/4, 25 3/4, 27, 28 1/2, 29 3/4, 31 1/4, 32 1/2)"

37 1/4 (39 1/2, 41 1/2, 43 3/4, 46, 48 1/4, 50 1/4, 52 1/2, 54 3/4)"

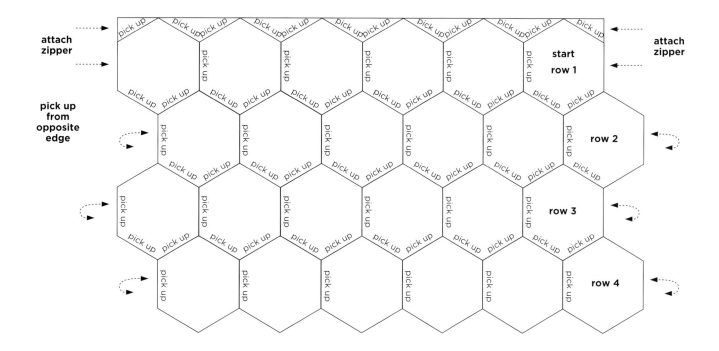

ROW 3 HEXAGONS

Using dpn, CO 32 (34, 36, 38, 40, 42, 44, 46, 48) sts each on Needles 1 and 2; using Needle 3, CO 16 (17, 18, 19, 20, 21, 22, 23, 24) sts, pick up and knit 16 (17, 18, 19, 20, 21, 22, 23, 24) sts along left-hand bottom edge of first Hexagon in Row 2—96 (102, 108, 114, 120, 126, 132, 138, 144) sts. Join for working in the rnd, being careful not to twist sts; pm after every 16 (17, 18, 19, 20, 21, 22, 23, 24) sts—this marks the 6 sides of the Hexagon.

Shape Hexagon: Begin St st, *work one Decrease Rnd. Work two rounds even; repeat from * until 2 (3, 2, 3, 2, 3, 2, 3, 2) sts remain between markers—12 (18, 12, 18, 12, 18, 12, 18, 12) sts total. Work 1 (2, 1, 2, 1, 2, 1, 2, 1) rnds even. Next rnd, *k2tog; repeat from * around—6 (9, 6, 9, 6, 9, 6, 9, 6) sts remain. Break yarn, thread through remaining sts, pull tight and fasten off.

Work 5 more Hexagons as follows: CO 16 (17, 18, 19, 20, 21, 22, 23, 24) sts for each of the 3 unattached sides and pick up and knit 16 (17, 18, 19, 20, 21, 22, 23, 24) sts each along bottom edges of Hexagon in Row 2 and left-hand edge of preceding Hexagon, dividing sts evenly among needles so that there are 2 full sides per needle—96 (102, 108, 114, 120, 126, 132, 138, 144) sts. Complete as for first Hexagon in Row 3.

ROW 4 HEXAGONS

Using dpn, CO 34 (36, 38, 40, 42, 44, 46, 48, 50) sts each on Needles 1 and 2; using Needle 3, CO 17 (18, 19, 20, 21, 22, 23, 24, 25) sts, pick up and knit 17 (18, 19, 20, 21, 22, 23, 24, 25) sts along right-hand bottom edge of first Hexagon in Row 3—102 (108, 114, 120, 126, 132, 138, 144, 150) sts. Join for working in the rnd, being careful not to twist sts; pm after every 17 (18, 19, 20, 21, 22, 23, 24, 25) sts—this marks the 6 sides of the Hexagon for each Hexagon.

Shape Hexagon: Begin St st, *work one Decrease Rnd. Work two rounds even; repeat from * until 3 (2, 3, 2, 3, 2, 3, 2, 3) sts remain between markers—18 (12, 18, 12, 18, 12, 18, 12, 18) sts total. Work 2 (1, 2, 1, 2, 1, 2, 1, 2) rnds even. Next rnd, *k2tog; repeat from * around—9 (6, 9, 6, 9, 6, 9, 6, 18) sts remain. Break yarn, thread through remaining sts, pull tight and fasten off.

Work 5 more Hexagons as follows: CO 17 (18, 19, 20, 21, 22, 23, 24, 25) sts for the 3 unattached sides and pick up and knit 17 (18, 19, 20, 21, 22, 23, 24, 25) sts along bottom edges of Hexagon in Row 3 and left-hand edge of preceding Hexagon, dividing sts evenly among needles so that there are 2 full sides per needle—102 (108, 114, 120, 126, 132, 138, 144, 150) sts. Complete as for first Hexagon in Row 4.

FINISHING

Waistband: With WS of piece facing, using circ needle, pick up and knit 132 (142, 151, 161, 170, 180, 189, 199, 208) sts along top edge of Waist Triangles; DO NOT JOIN. Knit 2 rows. BO all sts knitwise. Turn piece so Rev St st side is now facing out. Sew first and sixth Hexagons from Rows 2, 3 and 4 together on the Rev St st side (to match pick-up ridges), as indicated in assembly diagram. With St st side facing, stitch zipper to Zipper Edge Triangles and Row 1 Hexagons as indicated in assembly diagram; stitch hook and eye closure to top edge of zipper opening (optional).

Bottom Trim: With Rev St st side facing and using circ needle, pick up and knit 17 (18, 19, 20, 21, 22, 23, 24, 25) sts along each side of each Row 4 Hexagon, plus one st at each Hexagon point—108 (114, 120, 126, 132, 138, 144, 150, 156) sts. BO all sts knitwise.

Hex Afghan

I like to keep my design sense moving forward, and I'm constantly searching magazines, catalogs, and the Internet for details to add to my design vocabulary. Almost any visual medium is fair game. While planning this book, I found myself newly attuned to related shapes in the world around me. I saw hexagons seemingly everywhere, from columns of basalt on a beach in Iceland to a wasp nest attached to my own front porch. I found them in floor tiles, decorative windows from India, and textiles as well.

In my search for modern detailing to use in this book, I tripped across a photo of a beautiful cashmere throw. The original had permanently pressed pleats forming diamonds and chevrons, but somehow my mind made the leap to hexagons. (Cut a diamond in half, insert a couple of straight sides, and there you go—a hexagon.) My knitted afghan isn't pleated; instead, the knit and purl planes echo the feeling of the pressed fabric. Periodically adding rows of elongated hexagons, also inspired by the woven fabric, adds another level of interest.

NOTES

▶ *Fringe:* With RS of piece facing, insert crochet hook just above edge to receive Fringe, from back to front; catch the folded strands of yarn with the hook and pull through work to form a loop, insert ends of yarn through loop and pull to tighten. Cut loops at end of Fringe so all strands are loose.

BLANKET

CO 199 sts.

Establish Pattern:

Row 1 (RS) and all RS rows: Slip 2 sts purlwise, work Chart over 195 sts, k2.

Row 2 and all WS rows: Slip 2 sts purlwise, work as established to last 2 sts, p2.

Work even until piece measures approximately 54", ending with Row 8, 20, 32 or 52. BO all sts.

FRINGE

Cut 80 2-yard lengths of yarn. Fold each length in half 3 times. Work Fringe at each corner and every 5 sts along CO and BO edges. Using 3 strands from each Fringe, knot Fringe as shown in diagram. Trim ends even.

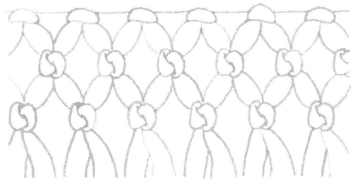

Knotted Fringe

SIZES
One size

FINISHED MEASUREMENTS
Approximately 50" wide × 54" long, before adding Fringe

YARN
Tahki Yarns Kerry (50% alpaca/50% wool; 90 yards/50 grams): 20 skeins #5026 rust

NEEDLES
One 32" (81 cm) circular (circ) needle size US 9 (5.5 mm)
Change needle size if necessary to obtain correct gauge.

NOTIONS
Crochet hook size US I/9 (5.5 mm) for Fringe

GAUGE
16 sts and 21 rows = 4" (10 cm) in Hexagon Pattern from Chart

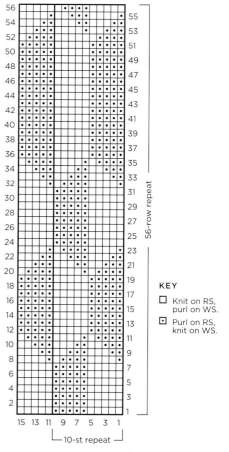

KEY

☐ Knit on RS, purl on WS.

⊡ Purl on RS, knit on WS.

Chapter 2

PENTAGONS*

* pentagon: (n) a closed figure with five straight sides

The pentagonal forms I studied occur in nature for a couple of different reasons. The first has to do with bubbles, and the second with a magical sequence of numbers we shall visit several times: the Fibonacci series.

As with hexagons, bubbles play an important role in the explanation of pentagons in nature. A single layer of bubbles arranges itself into hexagons, but a dry foam formed from multiple layers of bubbles—think of soapsuds—is composed of pentagonal and hexagonal faces. Foams can be very useful in the natural world; for instance, the foam of a spittle bug keeps its larvae from being seen, and hence eaten. The packing of bubbles in three dimensions may also help to explain the existence of a fairly newly discovered state of matter—quasicrystals, which defy the structural rules of crystals by possessing a unique five-fold symmetry (rather than six, as you can see in a snowflake) that allows them to pack together neatly to fill a space.

Pentagons are cool. As useful as hexagons are for covering a flat surface, they cannot cover a round surface—at least not without the help of a few pentagons. Exactly twelve pentagons are needed to close a shell whose other faces are hexagons, no matter how big the shell is.

The growth of leaves and flowers on plants is the subject of a later chapter, but an introduction to the subject applies here. It turns out that the number of petals or florets on a flower is most often a number from the Fibonacci series. This series of numbers was first defined by an Italian mathematician in 1202, but it relates to the "golden ratio" revered by the ancient Greeks as the harmonious, mystical constant of nature. The Fibonacci series starts with the numbers 0 and 1. Every subsequent number is derived by adding the two previous numbers: $0 + 1 = 1, 1 + 1 = 2, 1 + 2 = 3, 2 + 3 = 5, 3 + 5 = 8, 5 + 8 = 13, 8 + 13 = 21, 13 + 21 = 34$. The Fibonacci series starts out with this sequence: 0, 1, 1, 2, 3, 5, 8, 13, 21, 34, and goes on into infinity. Not only do most flowers have petals in numbers from the Fibonacci series, but many of these flowers have five petals, which gives them pentagonal symmetry.

For this chapter, I designed the Pentagon Aran Pullover and Cardigan (page 58) using pentagons simply as a surface decoration. Then I played with the three-dimensional shapes made by knitting pentagons together, forming both the Swirled Pentagon Pullover (page 46) and the Bubble Pullover (page 50). The Mosaic Shrug (page 64) plays with the open spaces between pentagons on a flat surface, while the Sand Dollar Pullover (page 42) and the Starfish Shawl (page 54) take advantage of the five-fold pattern repetition to create star and flower motifs.

FINISHED MEASUREMENTS
40 (44, 48, 52)" chest

YARN
Reynolds Yarns Rapture (50% silk/50% wool; 72 yards/50 grams): 11 (12, 14, 15) hanks #825 red clay

NEEDLES
One pair straight needles size US 7 (4.5 mm)

One pair straight needles size US 9 (5.5 mm)

One set of six double-pointed needles (dpn) size US 9 (5.5 mm)

Change needle size if necessary to obtain correct gauge.

NOTIONS
Row markers; stitch marker

GAUGE
16 sts and 21 rows = 4" (10 cm) in Stockinette st (St st) using larger needles

STITCH PATTERN
1×1 Rib:
(multiple of 2 sts; 1-row repeat)
All Rows: *K1, p1; repeat from * to end.

Sand Dollar Pullover

I see a sand dollar in this sweater, even though it wasn't my original intent. I was initially plant-inspired, envisioning leaves and little stems, repeated around. Some flowers and even creatures—like starfish, or the little sea urchin that is the sand dollar—are indeed pentagonal in nature. In fact, many patterns in nature have similar structures and appearances even though they are from divergent origins—plant versus animal. Scientists postulate that the basic laws of physics dictate complex forms with simple rules. How and when these laws come into play in an animal's or plant's development is still a mystery.

The movement from basic to complex is at work in this design, too. Any simple pattern, like the stem-and-leaf motif in this medallion, looks complicated when it's repeated five times around. The front of the pullover is constructed in several pieces around the center pentagonal medallion, while the sleeves and back are much more conventional.

NOTES

▶ **Stitch Pattern:** see left.

▶ **Kitchener Stitch:** Using a blunt yarn needle, thread a length of yarn approximately 4 times the length of the section to be joined. Hold the pieces to be joined wrong sides together, with the needles holding the stitches parallel, both ends pointing in the same direction. Working from right to left, *insert yarn needle in first stitch on front needle as if to knit, pull yarn through, remove st from needle; insert yarn needle into next st on front needle as if to purl, pull yarn through, leave st on needle; insert yarn needle into first st on back needle as if to purl, pull yarn through, remove st from needle; insert yarn needle into next st on back needle as if to knit, pull yarn through, leave st on needle. Repeat from *, working 3 or 4 stitches at a time, then go back and adjust tension to match the pieces being joined. When 1 st remains on each needle, cut yarn and pass through last 2 sts to fasten off.

BACK

Using smaller needles, CO 72 (80, 88, 96) sts; begin 1×1 Rib. Work even for 1½", ending with a WS row. (RS) Change to St st and larger needles. Work even until piece measures 12" from the beginning, ending with a WS row.

Shape Armholes: (RS) BO 3 sts at beginning of next 2 (2, 4, 4) rows, 2 sts at beginning of next 4 (6, 4, 6) rows, then decrease 1 st each side every other row 2 (2, 3, 3) times—54 (58, 62, 66) sts remain. Work even until armhole measures 7½ (8, 8½, 9)" from the beginning, ending with a WS row.

Shape Neck: (RS) Work 14 sts; join a second ball of yarn and BO center 26 (30, 34, 38) sts, work to end. Working BOTH SIDES AT SAME TIME, BO 4 sts at each neck edge 3 times—2 sts remain on each side for shoulders. Work even until armhole measures 9 (9½, 10, 10½)". BO all sts.

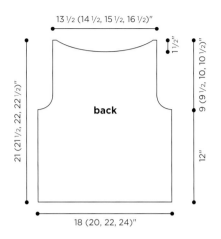

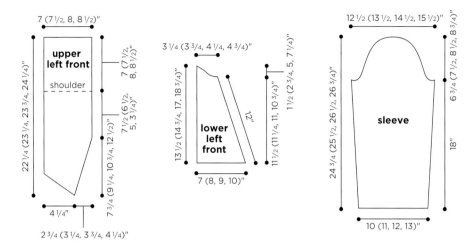

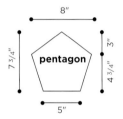

UPPER LEFT FRONT

Using larger needles, CO 2 sts. (RS) Begin St st, increase 1 st at beginning of row every 4 rows 10 (12, 14, 16) times, and AT THE SAME TIME, CO 2 sts at end of row every other row 8 times—28 (30, 32, 34) sts.

(RS) K1, m1, work to end—39 (31, 33, 35) sts. Work even until right-hand edge measures 7 ½ (6 ¾, 5, 3 ¼)" from last increase, ending with a WS row. (RS) Place marker (pm) at beginning of row for shoulder. Work even for 7 (7 ½, 8, 8 ½)", ending with a WS row. Place sts on holder for Back neck piece.

UPPER RIGHT FRONT

Work as for Upper Left Front, reversing shaping, until there are 28 (30, 32, 34) sts, ending with a WS row.

(RS) Work to last st, m1, k1—28 (30, 32, 34) sts. Continue as for Upper Left Front until shoulder marker; pm at end of row for shoulder. Complete as for Upper Left Front.

LOWER LEFT FRONT

Using smaller needles, CO 28 (32, 36, 40) sts; begin 1×1 Rib. Work even for 2 rows. Decrease Row (RS): Decrease 1 st at beginning of row every other row 1 (4, 9, 13) times, then every 4 rows 14 (13, 10, 8) times as follows: K1, k2tog, work to end, and AT THE SAME TIME, when piece measures 1 ½" from the beginning, change to larger needles and St st—13 (15, 17, 19) sts remain. Work even until shaping edge [not straight edge] measures 12" from the beginning, ending with a WS row.

Shape Armhole: (RS) BO 5 sts at beginning of row every other row 1 (0, 0, 0) time, 4 sts 0 (1, 1, 0) times, 3 sts once, then 2 sts 1 (1, 1, 2) times. Decrease 1 st at beginning of row every other row 1 (4, 2, 4) times, then every 4 rows 0 (0, 4, 6) times—2 sts remain. BO all sts.

LOWER RIGHT FRONT

Work as for Lower Left Front, reversing shaping and working Decrease Row as follows: Work to last 3 sts, ssk, k1.

LEAF INSERT CHART

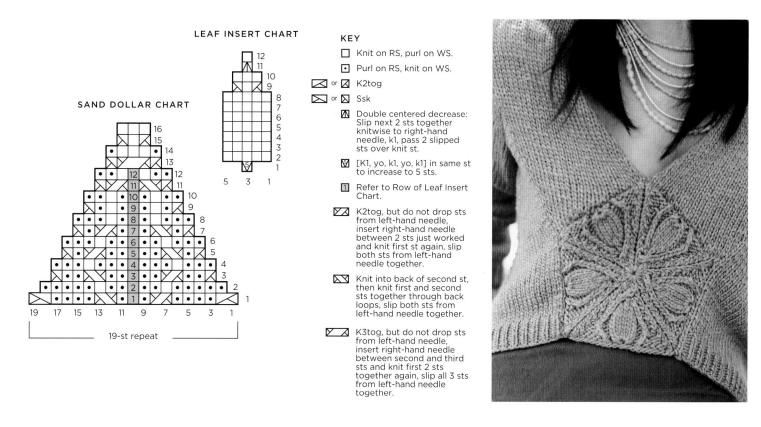

SAND DOLLAR CHART

19-st repeat

KEY

☐	Knit on RS, purl on WS.
☐•	Purl on RS, knit on WS.
⧄ or ⧄	K2tog
⧅ or ⧅	Ssk
⧊	Double centered decrease: Slip next 2 sts together knitwise to right-hand needle, k1, pass 2 slipped sts over knit st.
⧖	[K1, yo, k1, yo, k1] in same st to increase to 5 sts.
1	Refer to Row of Leaf Insert Chart.
⧄⧄	K2tog, but do not drop sts from left-hand needle, insert right-hand needle between 2 sts just worked and knit first st again, slip both sts from left-hand needle together.
⧅	Knit into back of second st, then knit first and second sts together through back loops, slip both sts from left-hand needle together.
⧄⧄⧄	K3tog, but do not drop sts from left-hand needle, insert right-hand needle between second and third sts and knit first 2 sts together again, slip all 3 sts from left-hand needle together.

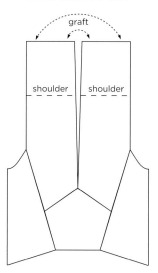

SLEEVES (make 2)

Using smaller needles, CO 40 (44, 48, 52) sts; begin 1×1 Rib. Work even for 1½", ending with a WS row. (RS) Change to St st and larger needles. Work even for 1", ending with a WS row.

Shape Sleeve: (RS) Increase 1 st each side every 14 rows 5 times as follows: K2, m1, work to last 2 sts, m1, k2—50 (54, 58, 62) sts. Work even until piece measures 18" from the beginning, ending with a WS row.

Shape Cap: (RS) BO 3 sts at beginning of next 2 rows, then 2 sts at beginning of next 2 rows. Decrease 1 st each side every other row twice, every 4 rows 5 (6, 7, 7) times, then every other row 1 (1, 1, 2) times as follows: K3, K2tog, work to last 5 sts, ssk, k3. BO 2 sts at beginning of next 2 rows, then 3 sts at beginning of next 2 rows—14 (16, 18, 20) sts remain. BO all sts.

PENTAGON

Using larger needles, CO 95 sts and divide evenly among 5 dpn (19 sts each). Join for working in the rnd, being careful not to twist sts; pm for beginning of rnd. Knit 1 rnd. Begin Sand Dollar Chart, working decreases as indicated—15 sts remain (3 sts each needle). Break yarn, thread through remaining sts, pull tight and fasten off.

FINISHING

Sew Upper Fronts to top edges of Pentagon [see assembly diagram]. Sew Lower Fronts to Pentagon and Upper Fronts. Graft sts of Upper Right and Left Fronts together using Kitchener st. Sew portion of Upper Fronts between markers to Back neck edge. Set in Sleeves. Sew side and Sleeve seams. Block lightly with steam.

ASSEMBLY DIAGRAM

graft

shoulder | shoulder

Swirled Pentagon Pullover

In a kind of geometry exercise, I discovered that six pentagons make a really nice yoke. You'll remember that pentagons can't fit together to fill a flat space, but what they can form is a curve. In this pullover, that curve fits perfectly around the shoulders. I inserted an extra three-fifths of a pentagon at the back neck to raise the collar for a better fit, preventing extra folds at the front neck. These spiraling pentagons are perfect for scarves and capelets, too (you'll see a similar construction in the Spiral Scarf on page 74). The knit one, purl one rib pattern looks great on both sides of a project and provides a self-finished edge, and the pentagon shaping is very easy to remember—by decreasing at the same five points the same way every round, you not only create a perfect pentagon, but the rib pattern creates a beautiful swirl as well.

NOTES

▶ *Stitch Patterns:* see right.

▶ CO using a tail method. For each Pentagon where you will pick up sts from an existing piece, make sure that your tail is long enough to complete the CO's and pick up's around the entire edge. When you pick up sts following a CO, pick up the first st with the tail end and the next st with the ball end; alternate this way across the entire pick up section.

BACK AND FRONT

Using smaller needles, CO 82 (90, 100, 108, 118) sts; begin 1×1 Rib. Work even for 1″. Change to larger needles and St st. Work even until piece measures 12 ½″ from the beginning, ending with a WS row.

Shape Armholes: BO 4 sts at beginning of next 0 (0, 2, 2, 4) rows, 3 sts at beginning of next 2 (4, 4, 4, 4) rows, 2 sts at the beginning of next 4 (4, 2, 2, 0) rows, then decrease 1 st each side 1 (0, 0, 0, 0) times—66 (70, 76, 84, 90) sts remain. Work 1 row even.

Shape Yoke Base: [Place marker (pm) between center two sts]. (RS) Ssk, work to marker, join a second ball of yarn and work to last 2 sts, k2tog. Work 1 row even. Working BOTH SIDES AT SAME TIME, work 1 row even. (RS) Decrease 1 st each side every other row 0 (0, 1, 2, 2) times, and AT THE SAME TIME, BO 2 sts at each neck edge 7 times, then decrease 1 st at each neck edge every other row 0 (1, 2, 3, 4) times—18 (19, 20, 22, 24) sts remain each side for Yoke base. BO remaining sts.

SLEEVES (make 2)

Using smaller needles, CO 36 (38, 40, 42, 44) sts; begin 1×1 Rib. Work even for 2 ½″. Change to larger needles and St st. Work even for 1″, ending with a WS row.

Shape Sleeve: (RS) Increase 1 st each side this row, every 8 rows 0 (0, 0, 5, 10) times, every 10 rows 0 (3, 9, 5, 1) times, then every 12 rows 7 (5, 0, 0, 0) times as follows: K2, m1, k to last 2 sts, m1, k2—52 (56, 60, 64, 68) sts. Work even until piece measures 18″ from the beginning, ending with a WS row.

Shape Cap: (RS) BO 3 sts at beginning of next 2 rows, 2 sts at beginning of next 2 rows. Decrease 1 st each side every other row 3 times, every 4 rows 4 (5, 5, 6, 6) times, then every other row 2 (2, 3, 3, 4) times, as follows: k2, k2tog, knit to last 4 sts, ssk, k2. BO 2 sts at beginning of next 2 rows, then 3 sts at beginning of next 2 rows—14 (16, 18, 20, 22) sts remain. BO all sts.

SIZES
Petite (Small, Medium, Large, X-Large)
Shown in size Small

FINISHED MEASUREMENTS
36 ½ (40, 44 ½, 48, 52 ½)″ chest

YARN
Berroco Pleasure (66% angora, 29% merino wool, 5% nylon; 130 yards/50 grams): 10 (11, 13, 14, 15) balls #8617 verdigris

NEEDLES
One pair straight needles size US 6 (4 mm)
One pair straight needles size US 8 (5 mm)
One 16″ (40 cm) circular (circ) needle size US 6 (4 mm)
One set of six double-pointed needles (dpn) size US 9 (5.5 mm)
Change needle size if necessary to obtain correct gauge.

NOTIONS
Stitch markers

GAUGE
18 sts and 25 rows = 4″ (10 cm) in Stockinette st (St st) using larger needles

STITCH PATTERNS
1×1 Rib:
(multiple of 2 sts; 1-row repeat)
All Rows: *K1, p1; repeat from * across.

2×2 Rib:
(multiple of 4 sts; 1-rnd repeat)
All Rnds: *K2, p2; repeat from * around.

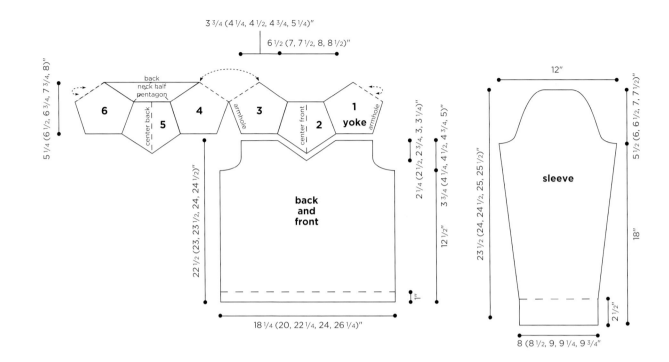

YOKE

You may either work entire Yoke independent of Front and Back pieces and sew finished Yoke on afterwards, or pick up sts from Front and Back as you go. Instructions for both options are given below.

Independent Yoke:

Pentagon 1: Using dpn, CO 20 (22, 24, 26, 28) sts on each of 5 needles—100 (110, 120, 130, 140) sts total. Join for working in the rnd, being careful not to twist sts; place marker (pm) for beginning of rnd. *P1, k1; repeat from * around.

Shape Pentagon: Continuing in Rib, work Decrease Rnd as follows: *Work to last 2 sts on needle, k2tog; repeat from * around. Repeat Decrease Rnd until 2 sts remain on each needle. Break yarn, thread through remaining sts, pull tight and fasten off. Work next four Pentagons as follows: CO 80 (88, 96, 104, 112) sts on each of 4 needles; on Needle 5, pick up and knit 20 (22, 24, 26, 28) sts from one side of previous Pentagon, as indicated on schematic. Work as for Pentagon 1. Work sixth Pentagon as follows: CO 40 (44, 48, 52, 56) sts on 2 needles; on Needle 3, pick up and knit 20 (22, 24, 26, 28) sts from one side of first Pentagon; on Needle 4, CO 20 (22, 24, 26, 28) sts; on Needle 5, pick up and knit 20 (22, 24, 26, 28) sts from one side of fifth Pentagon, as indicated on schematic. Work as for Pentagon 1.

Picked Up Yoke:

Pentagon 1: Using dpn, CO 20 (22, 24, 26, 28) sts on each of 4 needles; on Needle 5, pick up and knit 20 (22, 24, 26, 28) sts along left top of Front Yoke base—100 (110, 120, 130, 140) sts total. *P1, k1; repeat from * around.

Shape Pentagon as for Independent Yoke.

Pentagon 2: CO 20 (22, 24, 26, 28) sts on each of 2 needles; on Needle 3, pick up and knit 20 (22, 24, 26, 28) sts along left side of Pentagon 1; on Needles 4 and 5, pick up and knit 20 (22, 24, 26, 28) sts each along left and right edges of Yoke base shaping—100 (110, 120, 130, 140) sts. Work as for Pentagon 1.

Pentagon 3: CO 20 (22, 24, 26, 28) sts on each of 3 needles; on Needle 4, pick up and knit 20 (22, 24, 26, 28) sts along left side of Pentagon 2; on Needle 5, pick up and knit 20 (22, 24, 26, 28) sts along right top of Yoke base—100 (110, 120, 130, 140) sts. Work as for Pentagon 1.

Pentagon 4: CO 20 (22, 24, 26, 28) sts on each of 2 needles; on Needle 3, pick up and knit 20 (22, 24, 26, 28) sts from top side of Pentagon 3 (this forms the right shoulder seam); on Needle 4, CO 20 (22, 24, 26, 28) sts on Needle 5, pick up and knit 20 (22, 24, 26, 28) sts along right top of Back Yoke base—100 (110, 120, 130, 140) sts. Work as for Pentagon 1.

Pentagon 5: Work as for Pentagon 2.

Pentagon 6: CO 20 (22, 24, 26, 28) sts on 1 needle; on Needle 2, pick up and knit 20 (22, 24, 26, 28) sts from top side of Pentagon 1 (this forms the left shoulder seam); on Needle 3, CO 20 (22, 24, 26, 28) sts; on Needle 4, pick up and knit 20 (22, 24, 26, 28) sts along left side of Pentagon 5; on Needle 5, pick up and knit 20 (22, 24, 26, 28) sts along left top of Yoke base—100 (110, 120, 130, 140) sts. Work as for Pentagon 1.

Back Neck: Work half Pentagon along Back Yoke Pentagons as follows: Using dpn, pick up and knit 20 (22, 24, 26, 28) sts along on left side of Pentagon 4; on Needle 2, pick up and knit 20 (22, 24, 26, 28) sts along top of Pentagon 5; on Needle 3, pick up and knit 21 (23, 25, 27, 29) sts along right side of Pentagon 6—61 (67, 73, 79, 85) sts. DO NOT JOIN. Work in 1×1 Rib to last st, end k1. Row 1 (RS): Continuing in 2×2 Rib, on Needle 1, *work to last 2 sts, k2tog*, on Needle 2, repeat between *, on Needle 3, work to last 3 sts, k2tog, p1. Row 2: On Needle 1, k1, p2tog, rib to end, on Needle 2, *p2tog, work to end*, on Needle 3, repeat between *. Repeat Rows 1 and 2 until 6 sts remain on Needles 1 and 2 and 7 sts remain on Needle 3. Break yarn and thread through remaining sts, pull tight and fasten off.

FINISHING

Sew Yoke to Front and Back (if you didn't knit it on). Set in Sleeves. Sew side and Sleeve seams.

Neckband: Using circ needle, beginning at left shoulder seam, pick up and knit 84 (92, 100, 108, 116) sts around neck shaping. Join for working in the rnd, being careful not to twist sts; place marker (pm) for beginning of rnd; begin 2×2 Rib. Work even for 9". BO all sts.

Bubble Pullover

Theoretical mathematicians postulate about the "perfect" foam, a grouping of bubbles that exhibits the most stable structure with the smallest surface area possible. For a single bubble, the perfect structure is a sphere. When bubbles are packed together, with flat sides forming where the bubbles touch, they create a foam. In the "perfect" foam, many of these sides must be pentagons.

This pullover mimics and teases several of these "perfect foam" concepts. Instead of a grouping of bubbles that creates pentagons, it's a single, spherelike bubble that is made up of pentagons (as if one bubble has been plucked from the foam, sides intact). If you fold a series of pentagon shapes together so no holes remain, you're left with something close to a sphere. Try it yourself: Trace the figure in the assembly diagram onto a plain piece of paper and cut out around the heavy line. Fold it into a bubble shape with an open top and bottom. This is the basic structure of the bubble sweater.

The blouson shape of this pullover has an Eighties feel. A narrow (but not tight) sleeve keeps the overall look flattering even though the body is oversized.

SIZES
Small (Medium, Large)
Shown in size Medium

FINISHED MEASUREMENTS
Note: This pullover is very roomy and is sized to fit 34–38 (40–44, 46–50)" bust. Finished measurements 46 (51, 59)" chest at widest point.

YARN
Goddess Yarns Phoebe (100% baby alpaca; 73 yards/50 grams): 16 (19, 22) hanks #8126 wild aster

NEEDLES
One pair straight needles size US 7 (4.5 mm)

One pair straight needles size US 9 (5.5 mm)

One 16" (40 cm) circular (circ) needle size US 9 (5.5 mm)

One 24" (60 cm) circular needle size US 7 (4.5 mm)

One set of five 6" double-pointed needles (dpn) size 9 (5.5 mm)

Change needle size if necessary to obtain correct gauge.

NOTIONS
Stitch markers; six ¾" buttons

GAUGE
18 sts and 22 rows = 4" (10 cm) in Stockinette st (St st) using larger needles

STITCH PATTERN
2×2 Rib:
(multiple of 4 sts + 2; 2-row repeat)
Row 1 (WS): P2, *k2, p2; repeat from * to end.
Row 2: K2, *p2, k2; repeat from * to end.
Repeat Rows 1 and 2 for 2×2 Rib.

NOTES
▌ *Stitch Pattern:* see left.

▌ CO using a tail method. For each Pentagon where you will pick up sts from an existing piece, make sure that your tail is long enough to complete the CO's and pick up's around the entire edge. When you pick up sts following a CO, pick up the first st with the tail end and the next st with the ball end; alternate this way across the entire pick-up section.

BODY
PENTAGON 1

Note: Change to dpn when necessary for number of sts remaining.

Using larger circ needle, CO 160 (180, 200) sts. Join for working in the rnd, being careful not to twist sts; place marker (pm) for beginning of rnd, then after every 32 (36, 40) sts to mark 5 sides of Pentagon.

Rnds 1, 3 and 5: Knit.

Rnds 2, 4, 6 and 7: [K2tog, knit to 2 sts before next marker, ssk] 5 times—120 (140, 160) sts remain after Rnd 7.

Repeat Rnds 1–7 until 2 sts remain between markers (*NOTE: Sizes S and L will end with Rnd 6; Size M will end with Rnd 2*). Break yarn, thread through remaining sts, pull tight and fasten off.

PENTAGON 2

CO 128 (144, 160) sts, pick up and knit 32 (36, 40) sts along side A of Pentagon 1—160 (180, 200) sts. Work as for Pentagon 1.

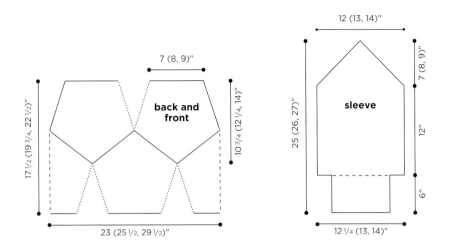

PENTAGON 3

CO 96 (108, 120) sts, pick up and knit 32 (36, 40) sts along side B of Pentagon 1 (see assembly diagram), and 32 (36, 40) sts along side B of Pentagon 2—160 (180, 200) sts. Work as for Pentagon 1.

PENTAGON 4

Work as for Pentagon 3, picking up sts along side A of Pentagons 3 and 2.

PENTAGON 5

Work as for Pentagon 2, picking up sts along side B of Pentagon 4 only; do not attach to Pentagon 3.

PENTAGON 6

Work as for Pentagon 3, picking up sts along side A of Pentagons 5 and 4.

PENTAGON 7

Work as for Pentagon 3, picking up sts along side B of Pentagons 5 and 6.

PENTAGON 8

CO 32 (36, 40) sts, pick up and knit 32 (36, 40) sts along side D of Pentagon 2, 32 (36, 40) sts along side E of Pentagon 1, 32 (36, 40) sts along side A of Pentagon 7, and 32 (36, 40) sts along side A of Pentagon 6—160 (180, 200) sts. Work as for Pentagon 1.

SLEEVES (make 2)

Using smaller needles, CO 38 (42, 46) sts; begin 2×2 Rib. Work even for 6″, increase 17 sts evenly spaced across last (WS) row—55 (59, 63) sts. Change to larger needles and St st. Work even until piece measures 18″ from the beginning, ending with a WS row. Pm at each end for armhole.

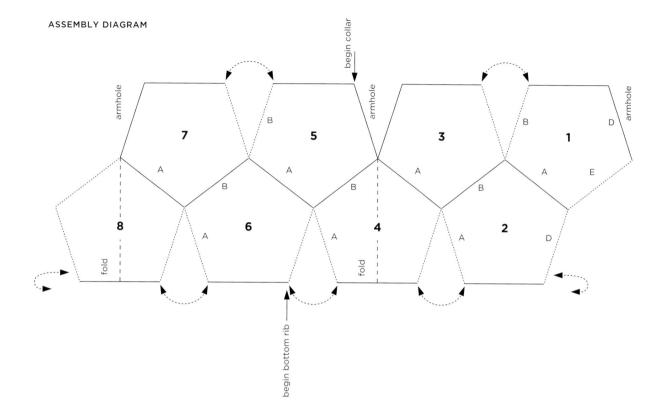

Shape Cap: (RS) Continuing in St st, decrease 2 sts each side every other row 6 (5, 4) times as follows: K1, k3tog, knit to last 4 sts, sssk, k1—31 (39, 47) sts remain. Work 1 WS row even. (RS) Decrease 1 st each side every other row 13 (17, 21) times as follows: K1, k2tog, knit to last 3 sts, ssk, k1—5 sts remain. Work 1 WS row even. Next row (RS), k1, slip 2 sts tog as if to k2tog, k1, psso, k1. BO remaining 3 sts.

BOTTOM RIB

Using smaller needles and beginning at lower right corner of Pentagon 6 as indicated on assembly diagram, pick up and knit 40 (44, 48) sts along bottom edge of each Pentagon—160 (176, 192) sts. Next row (WS), CO 6 sts; begin 2×2 Rib, beginning with k2—166 (182, 198) sts. Work even until ribbing measures 1″, ending with a WS row. (RS) Make 1 buttonhole as follows: Work to last 6 sts, ssk, yo, p2, k2. Work even until ribbing measures 4¼″ from the beginning, making a second buttonhole when ribbing measures 3″ from the beginning. BO all sts loosely in ribbing.

FINISHING

Sew in Sleeves. Sew Sleeve seams. ***Collar:*** Using smaller circ needle and beginning at armhole edge of Pentagon 5 as indicated on assembly diagram, pick up and knit 31 (35, 39) sts across top of first Pentagon, 32 (36, 40) sts across each of the next 2 Pentagons, then 31 (35, 39) sts across last Pentagon—126 (142, 158) sts; DO NOT JOIN. (WS) Begin 2×2 Rib, beginning with k2. Continuing in 2×2 Rib as established, make 1 buttonhole on RS at 1″ and every 2½″ thereafter as follows: P2, k2, yo, p2tog, work to end. When Collar measures 10″ from the beginning, BO all sts loosely in ribbing. Sew on buttons opposite buttonholes.

Starfish Shawl

In nature, the most rudimentary laws of physics can result in complex patterns. With that in mind, I tried to pare down each of the three major elements in this design to its most basic form. The first element is the pentagonal structure. The easiest way to shape a pentagon is to knit two stitches together in the same five locations every single row, so that's what I chose. For the secondary element—the surface embellishment—I wanted a lace pattern. I settled on a simple diagonal openwork with easy-to-memorize stitch and row repeats. The five-pointed star formed by the Stockinette stitch center is a bonus pattern, a welcome surprise. The arm-hole slits are the third element of this design (for those of us who have trouble keeping a shawl on). To make the slits most easily, four Garter stitches are placed next to each rib formed by the decreases; the arm slit cuts this in half, leaving two Garter stitches on each self-finished edge.

This shawl can be worn in many different ways. Place the short section toward the top in back if you just want to hang it on your arms. Or, with the larger section on top, wrap it around to the front and secure it with a stick or pin, then have fun playing with the resulting voluminous shawl collar.

SIZES
One Size

FINISHED MEASUREMENTS
46" wide

YARN
Harrisville Designs Cashmere Blend (50% cashmere/50% wool; 190 yards/50 grams): 6 hanks #227 taupe

NEEDLES
One 24" (60 cm) circular (circ) needle size US 6 (4 mm)

One 16" (40 cm) circular needle size US 6 (4 mm)

One set of six 6" double-pointed needles (dpn) size US 6 (4 mm)

Change needle size if necessary to obtain correct gauge.

GAUGE
21 sts and 30 rows = 4" (10 cm) in Stockinette st (St st)

NOTIONS
Stitch markers

STITCH PATTERN
Garter Stitch in-the-Round:
(any number of sts; 2-rnd repeat)
Rnd 1: Knit.
Rnd 2: Purl.
Repeat Rnds 1 and 2 for Garter St.

NOTES

❯ *Stitch Pattern:* see left.

SHAWL

Note: Change to shorter circ needle, then to dpn when necessary for number of sts remaining.

Using longer circ needle, CO 730 sts. Join for working in the rnd, being careful not to twist sts; place marker (pm) for beginning of rnd. Begin Garter St in-the-Round. Work even for 5 rnds. Place marker every 146 sts. This will divide the work into 5 equal sections.

Establish Pattern: (RS) *Work Sts 1–3 of Chart once, Pattern A once, Pattern B 25 times, then work to end of Chart; repeat from * 4 times. When all 10 rows of Chart are complete, continue as indicated on Chart and in Chart Notes. Work even until piece measures 4" from the beginning, ending with an even-numbered rnd.

Split for Armhole: Work to end of Section 2; join a second ball of yarn and work to end. Turn and work to beginning of Section 1. Working back and forth AT SAME TIME on Sections 1 and 2 with one ball of yarn and Sections 3, 4 and 5 with a separate ball of yarn, work even for 8", ending with an even-numbered row. Joining Rnd: Work even on all 5 Sections. Continue as established until 10 sts remain (2 sts each Section). Break yarn, thread through remaining sts, pull tight and fasten off.

Block piece to measurements.

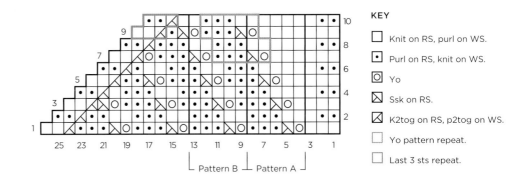

CHART NOTES

1. Yo pattern moves 1 st to the left on every odd-numbered rnd, as indicated in blue box.

2. After working the first 10 rows of the Chart, continue as established, working 2 Garter sts at beginning of each Section, then working in St st to first yo. Work in yo pattern from chart (in blue box) to last 3 sts, work as indicated in red box. Note that last pattern repeat may be incomplete.

3. When working back and forth for Armholes, refer to chart for decreases on WS rows.

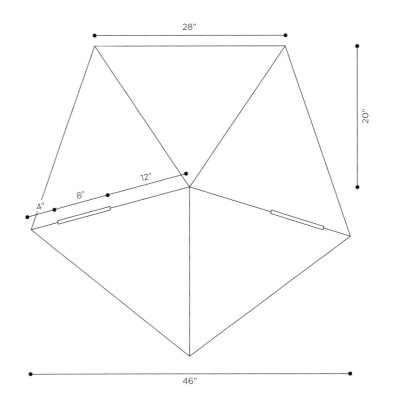

Pentagon Aran Pullover and Cardigan

Perhaps more conventional in construction than other pieces in this volume, these sibling sweaters have the look of traditional Arans. It's only upon close inspection that the pentagons become evident. It feels like a children's game, or maybe something from an IQ test—how many different shapes can you find in this picture? Like the sweater, the pentagon motif itself utilizes a trick of the eye—it's not forced too strictly on this surface design. Gently sloping cables define the outline of double-stacked pentagons, with horizontal lines left to the imagination. After playing around with garter ridges as a way of defining the fifth side, I decided I preferred the "incomplete" version, letting the eye complete the pentagon.

ARAN PULLOVER

NOTES

▶ *Stitch Pattern:* see right.

BACK

Using larger needles, CO 100 (112, 124, 136) sts; begin pattern from Chart, as indicated for your size. Work even until piece measures 19½ (20, 20½, 21)" from the beginning, ending with a WS row.

Shape Neck: (RS) Work 40 (45, 50, 55) sts; join a second ball of yarn and BO center 20 (22, 24, 26) sts, work to end. Working BOTH SIDES AT SAME TIME, BO 5 sts at each neck edge twice—30 (35, 40, 45) sts remain each side for shoulders. BO remaining sts.

FRONT

Work as for Back until piece measures 17½" from the beginning, ending with a WS row.

Shape Neck: (RS) Work 41 (46, 51, 56) sts; join a second ball of yarn and BO center 18 (20, 22, 24) sts, work to end. Working BOTH SIDES AT SAME TIME, BO 4 sts at each neck edge once, 3 sts once, 2 sts once, then decrease 1 st every other row twice—30 (35, 40, 45) sts remain each side for shoulders. Work even until piece measures same as for Back to shoulder. BO all sts.

SLEEVES (make 2)

Using smaller needles, CO 40 (42, 44, 46) sts; begin 1×1 Rib. Work even for 2". (RS) Change to larger needles and St st. Work even for 1", ending with a WS row.

Shape Sleeve: (RS) Increase 1 st each side every 6 rows 1 (5, 9, 13) times, then every 8 rows 12 (9, 6, 3) times as follows: K2, m1, knit to last 2 sts, m1, k2—66 (70, 74, 78) sts. Work even until piece measures 20" from the beginning. BO all sts.

FINISHING

Sew shoulder seams. Measure down 8¼ (8¾, 9¼, 9¾)" from shoulder seam along each side and place markers. Sew Sleeves between markers. Sew side and Sleeve seams. *Neckband:* Using smaller needles, beginning at left shoulder seam, pick up and knit 96 (100, 104, 108) sts around neck shaping. Join for working in the round, being careful not to twist sts; place marker (pm) for beginning of rnd. Begin 1×1 Rib. Work even for 10". BO all sts in pattern.

ARAN PULLOVER ONLY
(for Aran Cardigan, see page 62)

SIZES
Small (Medium, Large, X-Large)
Shown in size Small

FINISHED MEASUREMENTS
40 (45, 50, 55)" chest

YARN
Jo Sharp Silk Road Aran (85% wool/10% silk/5% cashmere; 95 yards/50 grams): 14 (15, 16, 18) balls #128 heather

NEEDLES
One pair straight needles size US 6 (4 mm)
One pair straight needles size US 8 (5 mm)
One 16" (40 cm) circular (circ) needle size US 6 (4 mm)
Change needle size if necessary to obtain correct gauge.

NOTIONS
Stitch marker

GAUGE
16 sts and 24 rows = 4" (10 cm) in Stockinette st (St st) using larger needles
24 sts and 34 rows = 5" (12.75 cm) in center repeat from Chart using larger needles

STITCH PATTERN
1×1 Rib:
(multiple of 2 sts; 1-row repeat)
All Rows/Rnds: *K1, p1; repeat from * to end of row/rnd.

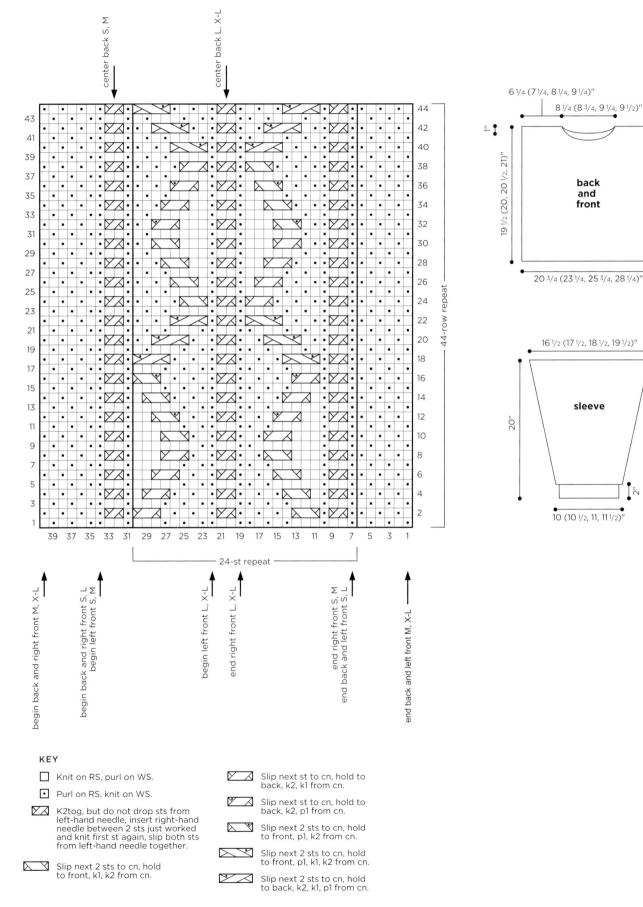

KEY

☐ Knit on RS, purl on WS.

⊡ Purl on RS, knit on WS.

▨ K2tog, but do not drop sts from left-hand needle, insert right-hand needle between 2 sts just worked and knit first st again, slip both sts from left-hand needle together.

▱ Slip next 2 sts to cn, hold to front, k1, k2 from cn.

▱ Slip next st to cn, hold to back, k2, k1 from cn.

▱ Slip next st to cn, hold to back, k2, p1 from cn.

▱ Slip next 2 sts to cn, hold to front, p1, k2 from cn.

▱ Slip next 2 sts to cn, hold to front, p1, k1, k2 from cn.

▱ Slip next 2 sts to cn, hold to back, k2, k1, p1 from cn.

ARAN CARDIGAN ONLY
(for Aran Pullover, see page 59)

SIZES
Small (Medium, Large, X-Large)
Shown in size Medium

FINISHED MEASUREMENTS
41½ (46½, 51½, 56½)" chest

YARN
Jo Sharp Silk Road Aran Tweed
(85% wool/10% silk/5% cashmere;
93 yards/50 gram): 14 (15, 16, 18)
balls #115 wintergrass

NEEDLES
One pair straight needles size US 6
(4 mm)

One pair straight needles size US 8
(5 mm)

One 16" (40 cm) circular (circ)
needle size US 6 (4 mm)

Change needle size if necessary to
obtain correct gauge.

NOTIONS
Stitch markers; matching 24 (24, 26,
26)" separating zipper. *NOTE: These
are standard zipper lengths, but you
may special order custom lengths as
well, if you choose to change the
length of the sweater.*

GAUGE
16 sts and 24 rows = 4" (10 cm) in
Stockinette st (St st) using larger
needles

24 sts and 34 rows = 5" (12.75 cm) in
center repeat from Chart using larger
needles

STITCH PATTERN
1×1 Rib:
(multiple of 2 sts; 1-row repeat)
All Rows: *K1, p1; repeat from * to
end.

ARAN CARDIGAN

NOTES
▶ *Stitch Pattern:* see left.

BACK
Using larger needles, CO 100 (112, 124, 136) sts; begin pattern from Chart, as indicated for your size. Work even until piece measures 23½ (24, 24½, 25)" from the beginning, ending with a WS row.

Shape Neck: (RS) Work 40 (45, 50, 55) sts; join a second ball of yarn and BO center 20 (22, 24, 26) sts, work to end. Working BOTH SIDES AT SAME TIME, BO 5 sts at each neck edge twice—30 (35, 40, 45) sts remain each side for shoulders. BO remaining sts.

LEFT FRONT
Using larger needles, CO 52 (58, 64, 70) sts; begin pattern from Chart, as indicated for your size. Work even until piece measures 22½ (23, 23½, 24)" from the beginning, ending with a RS row.

Shape Neck: (WS) BO 11 (12, 13, 14) sts at neck edge once, 4 sts once, 3 sts once, 2 sts once, then decrease 1 st every other row twice—30 (35, 40, 45) sts remain. Work even until piece measures same as for Back to shoulder. BO all sts.

RIGHT FRONT
Work as for Left Front, beginning and ending where indicated on chart and reversing all shaping.

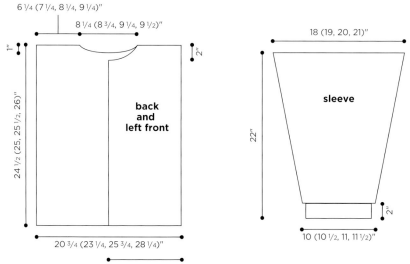

SLEEVES (make 2)

Using smaller needles, CO 40 (42, 44, 46) sts; (RS) begin 1×1 Rib. Work even for 2", ending with a WS row. (RS) Change to larger needles and St st. Work even for 1", ending with a WS row.

Shape Sleeve: (RS) Increase 1 st each side every 6 rows 4 (8, 12, 16) times, then every 8 rows 12 (9, 6, 3) times as follows: K2, m1, knit to last 2 sts, m1, k2—72 (76, 80, 84) sts. Work even until piece measures 22" from the beginning. BO all sts.

FINISHING

Sew shoulder seams. Measure down 9 (9 ½, 10, 10 ½)" from shoulder seam along each side and place markers. Sew Sleeves between markers. Sew side and Sleeve seams.

Neckband: Using circ needle, beginning at left shoulder seam, pick up and knit 87 (91, 95, 99) sts around neck shaping. Join for working in the rnd, being careful not to twist sts; place marker (pm) for beginning of rnd. Begin 1×1 Rib. Work even for 2". BO all sts in pattern. Sew in zipper.

Mosaic Shrug

Pentagons don't fit together to fill a flat surface. Hexagons, squares, and triangles will tile a flat plane without leaving gaps, but pentagons leave spaces, no matter how much you fiddle with them. This shrug, designed as a flat plane, plays around with those spaces. The diamond shapes between the pentagons are left open.

SIZES
One Size

FINISHED MEASUREMENTS
40" wide × 13" long

YARN
Reynolds Yarns Odyssey (100% merino wool; 104 yards/50 grams): 7 balls #442 rust mix

NEEDLES
One set of six double-pointed needles (dpn) size US 7 (4.5 mm)
Change needle size if necessary to obtain correct gauge.

NOTIONS
Stitch marker

GAUGE
20 sts and 25 rows = 4" (10 cm) in Stockinette st (St st)

NOTES

▶ *Decrease Rnd:* [K2tog, knit to 2 sts before end of needle, ssk] 5 times.

▶ CO using a tail method. For each Pentagon where you will pick up sts from an existing piece, make sure that your tail is long enough to complete the CO's and pick up's around the entire edge. When you pick up sts following a CO, pick up the first st with the tail end and the next st with the ball end; alternate this way across the entire pick up section.

SHRUG (made of 36 Pentagons)
PENTAGON

Using your preferred tail CO method, CO 80 sts; divide evenly among 4 needles. Join for working in the rnd, being careful not to twist sts; place marker (pm) for beginning of rnd. [Purl one rnd, work Decrease Rnd] twice. *Knit one rnd, work Decrease Rnd; repeat from * until 2 sts remain on each needle—10 sts total. Break yarn, thread through remaining sts, pull tight and fasten off.

Work subsequent Pentagons from existing Pentagons according to diagram, picking up 16 sts along attached sides and casting on 16 sts for unattached sides. The first and last three Pentagons and the Pentagons at each side of neck are attached to each other by picking up 2 sts at each corner (1 st on either side of the point), as noted on diagram.

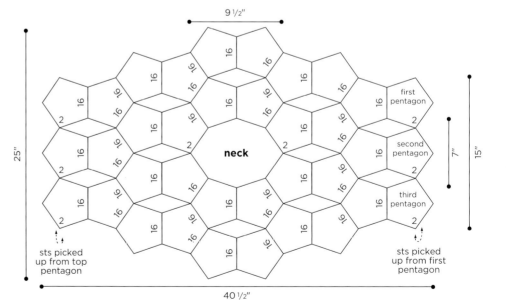

NOTE: The numbers within each pentagon indicate the number of sts to be picked up on the edge or corner indicated.

Chapter 3

SPIRALS*

* spiral: (n) a curve on a plane that winds around a fixed center point at a continuously increasing or decreasing distance from the point

ature makes spirals on many scales. Stars cluster and move slowly in spiral galaxies millions of light years across. The raging winds of hurricanes form spirals hundreds of miles wide. The spiral of a ram's horn is about a foot across, and the spiral of a seashell can be as small as a fraction of an inch.

Spirals can be transitory or fixed. The curve of an elephant's trunk, the curl of a monkey's or chameleon's tail—these are spirals that come and go at the creature's will. Certain chemical reactions can form constantly changing spiral waves, and chaotic fluids form wonderful transitory spirals. Conversely, a sheep's horn, a snail's shell, a beaver's tooth, and a cat's claw are solid and fixed in shape. Although their shape is fixed, they are still growing, being constantly added to at one end.

Some spirals increase in size at a steady speed, and some increase at a constant velocity, meaning the rate of *increase* of speed is constant. The first type, the spirals that increase at a constant speed, look like the spirals used for hypnosis in old movies or the spiral of a cinnamon bun. These are called spirals of Archimedes, and they aren't as common in nature as the second type, logarithmic spirals, which are formed by constant growth. A seashell or a horn becomes larger and larger at a constant rate as the creature making it grows. The original shape of the spiral remains but is expanded in all dimensions.

All six of the spiral knitted designs in this chapter are based on the ever-growing logarithmic spirals. I was inspired by the cross-section of a long shell for both the Cabled Spiral Pullover (page 82) and the Shell Tank (page 86). The Nautilus Poncho (page 70) is made from the small end to the large as a snail would make its shell, and it's specially shaped to fit on the shoulders before growing at a constant rate. The collar on the Ram's Horn Jacket (page 92) and the spiral on the cowl and sleeve of the Cowl Pullover (page 78) have a constant growth—perhaps not at a mathematically perfect logarithmic rate, but close enough to complete the illusion.

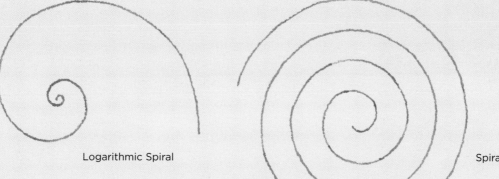

Logarithmic Spiral

Spiral of Archimedes

Nautilus Poncho

I knitted this poncho three times before I figured out the correct balance of mathematical accuracy and proper shoulder shaping. Once I got it right, I found the knitting to be a bit like eating potato chips—it goes quickly and it's so hard to stop. The poncho is made in a single Stockinette-stitch strip that widens as it lengthens, with short-row shaping at the shoulders. Keeping track of the short rows and increases is easy; I kept them at regular intervals. After the spiraling strip is completed, the piece is put together with basic crochet stitches, placed to further enhance the shell-like spiral structure. The instructions for both sizes are identical, only the gauge is different.

SIZES
To fit Teen (Adult)

FINISHED MEASUREMENTS
15 (19)" at widest point; 25 (28)" at longest point

YARN
Rowan Yarns Polar (60% pure new wool/30% alpaca/10% acrylic; 109 yards/100 grams): 4 balls #650 smirk (#643 blackforest)

NEEDLES
Teen Poncho: One pair straight needles size US 10½ (6.5 mm)
Adult Poncho: One pair straight needles size US 11 (8 mm)
Change needle size if necessary to obtain correct gauge.

NOTIONS
Teen Poncho: Crochet hook size US I/9
Adult Poncho: Crochet hook size US J/10

GAUGE
Teen Poncho: 14 sts and 19 rows = 4" (10 cm) in Stockinette st (St st)
Adult Poncho: 13 sts and 17 rows = 4" (10 cm) in St st

NOTES

▌ *Increase Row:* (RS) K1, m1, knit to end.

▌ To work the yo for the short rows, wrap the yarn over the top of the right-hand needle, from front to back, bringing the yarn back around to the front, ready to purl the next st.

PONCHO

CO 3 sts; begin St st (purl). Work even (knit 1 row, purl 1 row) for 28 rows. Next row (RS), work Increase Row. Work 1 row even.

Shape Poncho:

Short Row Section 1:

Rows 1 and 3 (RS): Knit.

Rows 2 and 4: Purl.

Row 5: K2, turn.

Row 6: Yo, purl to end.

Row 7: Work to yo, k2tog (yo and next st), knit to end.

Row 8: Purl.

Rows 9–24: Repeat Rows 1-8 twice.

Rows 25 and 27: Knit.

Rows 26 and 28: Purl.

Row 29: Work Increase Row—5 sts.

Row 30: Purl.

Repeat Rows 1–30 once—6 sts after Row 29.

Short Row Section 2:

Rows 1 and 3 (RS): Knit.

Rows 2 and 4: Purl.

Row 5: K3, turn.

Row 6: Yo, purl to end.

Row 7: Work to yo, k2tog (yo and next st), knit to end.

Row 8: Purl.

Rows 9–24: Repeat Rows 1-8 twice.

Rows 25 and 27: Knit.

Rows 26 and 28: Purl.

Row 29: Work Increase Row—7 sts.

Row 30: Purl.

Repeat Rows 1–30 once—8 sts after Row 29.

Short Row Section 3:

Rows 1 and 3 (RS): Knit.

Rows 2 and 4: Purl.

Row 5: K4, turn.

Row 6: Yo, purl to end.

Row 7: Work to yo, k2tog (yo and next st), knit to end.

Row 8: Purl.

Rows 9–24: Repeat Rows 1–8 twice.

Rows 25 and 27: Knit.

Rows 26 and 28: Purl.

Row 29: Work Increase Row—9 sts.

Row 30: Purl.

Repeat Rows 1–30 once—10 sts after Row 29.

*Work even for 30 rows. (RS) Work Increase Row. Work 1 row even. Repeat from * 11 times—22 sts. Work even for 17 rows. (WS) Knit 1 row. BO all sts knitwise. Fasten off, but do not break yarn.

FINISHING

Edging: Using crochet hook, working along left-hand edge, work 1 sc, *ch3, skip 3 rows, sc in next row; repeat from * to corner; along BO edge, work sc, ch3; along right-hand edge, work sc, *ch2, skip 2 rows, sc in next row; repeat from * to end of right-hand edge. Break yarn and fasten off.

Join: Mark 22" from beginning. Wrap beginning of strip to marker, forming a circle, with edges of RS's together. Join with a slip st. *Ch 2, sc into first loop of both edges, repeat from * to end.

Bottom Edging: Continuing with same yarn, *sc in first free loop of bottom edge, ch3; rep from * around bottom and across end.

6 1/4 (6 3/4)"

poncho

29 1/4 (35 1/4)"

51 1/4 (57 1/2)"

22"

3/4 (1)"

Spiral Scarf

This scarf defies categorization. The individual motifs are hexagons. The use of ribbing and decreasing is practically identical to that in the Swirled Pentagon Pullover (page 46). Yet the overall spiral construction trumps these other structures—the decreases even form secondary spirals. In order for the scarf to grow incrementally as it spirals, like a ram's horn or seashell, each new motif is one stitch smaller per side than the one before. The placement of each subsequent motif at a 120° angle forms the continual spiral. You may be tempted to add smaller and smaller hexagons, bringing the end to a sharp point. Or, by adding larger motifs at the other end, your scarf could grow as large as Dr. Dolittle's fictional sea snail.

NOTES

▶ Entire Scarf is worked using 2 strands of yarn held together.

▶ CO using a tail method. For each Hexagon where you will pick up sts from an existing piece, make sure that your tail is long enough to complete the CO's and pick up's around the entire edge. When you pick up sts following a CO, pick up the first st with the tail end and the next st with the ball end; alternate this way across the entire pick-up section.

▶ *Hexagon A:* [even # of sts per side] Using 2 strands of yarn held together, on Needle 1, *CO required number of sts for one side, place marker (pm), CO required number of sts for one side; repeat from * for Needle 2; for Needle 3, CO required number of sts for one side, pm, pick up and knit required number of sts for one side from side of preceding Hexagon. Join for working in the rnd, being careful not to twist sts; pm for beginning of rnd. *Establish Pattern:* *P1, k1; repeat from * around. *Shape Hexagon:* Decrease Rnd: *Work to 2 sts before marker, k2tog, work to last 2 sts on Needle, k2tog; repeat from * around—6 sts decreased each rnd. Repeat Decrease Rnd every rnd until 6 sts remain. Break yarn, thread through remaining sts, pull tight and fasten off.

▶ *Hexagon B:* [odd # of sts per side] Using 2 strands of yarn held together, on Needle 1, *CO required number of sts for one side, pm, CO required number of sts for one side; repeat for Needle 2; for Needle 3, CO required number of sts for one side, pm, pick up and knit required number of sts for one side from side of preceding Hexagon. Join for working in the rnd, being careful not to twist sts; pm for beginning of rnd. *Establish Pattern:* [*K1, p1; repeat from * to 1 st before marker, k1; **k1, p1; repeat from ** to last st on Needle, k1] for each Needle. *Shape Hexagon:* Decrease Rnd: *Work to 2 sts before marker, k2tog, work to last 2 sts on Needle, k2tog; repeat from * around—6 sts decreased each rnd. Repeat Decrease Rnd every rnd until 6 sts remain. Break yarn, thread through remaining sts, pull tight and fasten off.

SIZES
One size

FINISHED MEASUREMENTS
50" long along inside curve

YARN
Jade Sapphire 2-ply Mongolian Cashmere (100% cashmere; 400 yards/55 grams); 2 hanks everglades

NEEDLES
One set of four double-pointed needles (dpn) size US 4 (3.5 mm)

NOTIONS
Stitch markers; crochet hook size US E/4 (3.5 mm)

GAUGE
18 sts and 25 rows = 4" (10 cm) in 1×1 Rib using 2 strands of yarn held together

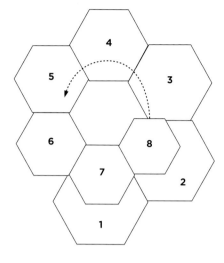

SCARF
HEXAGON 1

Using 2 strands of yarn held together, CO 22 sts per side [2 sides per needle]—132 sts. Complete as for Hexagon A.

HEXAGON 2

Using 2 strands of yarn held together, CO 21 sts for each of 5 sides, pick up and knit 21 sts along one side of Hexagon 1—126 sts. Complete as for Hexagon B.

HEXAGON 3

Using 2 strands of yarn held together, CO 20 sts for each of 5 sides, pick up and knit 20 sts along one side of Hexagon 2, 2 sides clockwise from where sts were picked up from Hexagon 1 [see assembly diagram]—100 sts. Complete as for Hexagon A.

REMAINING HEXAGONS

Work 12 more Hexagons. Each subsequent Hexagon will have 1 less st per side than the preceding. Complete as for either Hexagon A or B, depending on whether there are an even or odd number of sts per side.

FINISHING

Using crochet hook and 2 strands of yarn held together, work one row Sl St along inside edge of spiral.

Cowl Pullover

The sleeve, yoke, and cowl of this pullover are all knit in one big funnel, which is split open so that it can be attached to the body of the garment. The simple openwork pattern on the funnel section spirals around and around, the beginning of the row shifting over two stitches every round. The increases work quite gracefully as well. The spaces between the openwork become wider as more stitches are added, just as a seashell becomes wider as a mollusk grows.

NOTES

▌ *Stitch Pattern:* see right.

▌ When working Sleeve/Cowl, each rnd overlaps the previous rnd by 2 sts. Slip marker 2 sts to the left for new beginning of rnd. Increase rnds overlap preceding rnd by 3 sts. Move marker 3 sts to the left for new beginning of rnd.

▌ Sleeve/Cowl piece is worked in the rnd and then reinforced on a sewing machine before cutting slash for body opening.

BACK

Using smaller needles, CO 74 (82, 90, 98, 106) sts; begin 1×1 Rib. Work even for 3 rows. Change to larger needles and St st. Work even until piece measures 16″ from the beginning, ending with a WS row.

Shape Right Armhole Edge and Left Shoulder: (RS) BO 2 sts at beginning of next 10 (7, 7, 4, 4) rows. Work 0 (1, 1, 0, 0) (RS) rows even. (WS) BO 3 sts at beginning of row every other row 12 (16, 18, 22, 24) times—18 (20, 22, 24, 26) sts remain. BO 2 sts at beginning of next 4 RS rows, and AT THE SAME TIME, BO 2 (3, 3, 4, 4) sts at beginning of next 2 WS rows, then 3 (3, 4, 4, 5) sts at beginning of next 2 WS rows.

FRONT

Work as for Back, reversing all shaping.

LEFT SLEEVE

Using smaller needles, CO 42 (46, 50, 54, 58) sts; begin 1×1 Rib. Work even for 3 rows. Change to larger needles and St st. Work even for 2″, ending with a WS row.

Shape Sleeve: (RS) Continuing in St st, increase 1 st each side this row, then every 6 rows 11 times as follows: K2, m1, work to last 2 sts, m1, k2—66 (70, 74, 78, 82) sts. Work even until piece measures 17″ from the beginning, ending with a WS row.

Shape Cap: (RS) BO 2 sts at beginning of next 8 (22, 36, 35, 34) rows, then 3 sts at beginning of next 16 (8, 0, 2, 4) rows—2 sts remain. BO all sts.

RIGHT SLEEVE/COWL

Note: Change to 16″ and 24″ circ needle when work no longer fits on dpns.

Using dpn, CO 42 (46, 50, 54, 58) sts. Join for working in the rnd, being careful not to twist sts; place marker (pm) for beginning of rnd.

Establish Spiral Pattern: [K15 (17, 19, 21, 23) sts, yo, k1, yo, ssk, yo, [k2tog] twice] twice.

SIZES
Petite (Small, Medium, Large, X-Large)
Shown in size Small

FINISHED MEASUREMENTS
36 (40, 44, 48, 52)″ chest

YARN
Adrienne Vittadini Natasha (56% wool/17% alpaca/14% mohair; 72 yards/40 grams): 16 (18, 20, 22, 25) balls #22 lavender blue

NEEDLES
One pair straight needles size US 7 (4.5 mm)

One pair straight needles size US 9 (5.5 mm)

One set of five double-pointed needles (dpn) size US 9 (5.5 mm)

One 16″ (40 cm) circular (circ) needle size US 9 (5.5 mm)

One 24″ (60 cm) circular needle size US 9 (5.5 mm)

Change needle size if necessary to obtain correct gauge.

GAUGE
16 sts and 22 rows = 4″ (10 cm) in Stockinette st (St st) using larger needles

17 sts and 20 rows = 4″ (10 cm) in Spiral pattern using dpn, blocked

NOTIONS
Stitch marker; sewing needle and thread

STITCH PATTERN
1×1 Rib:
(multiple of 2 sts; 1-row repeat)
All Rows: *K1, p1; repeat from * to end.

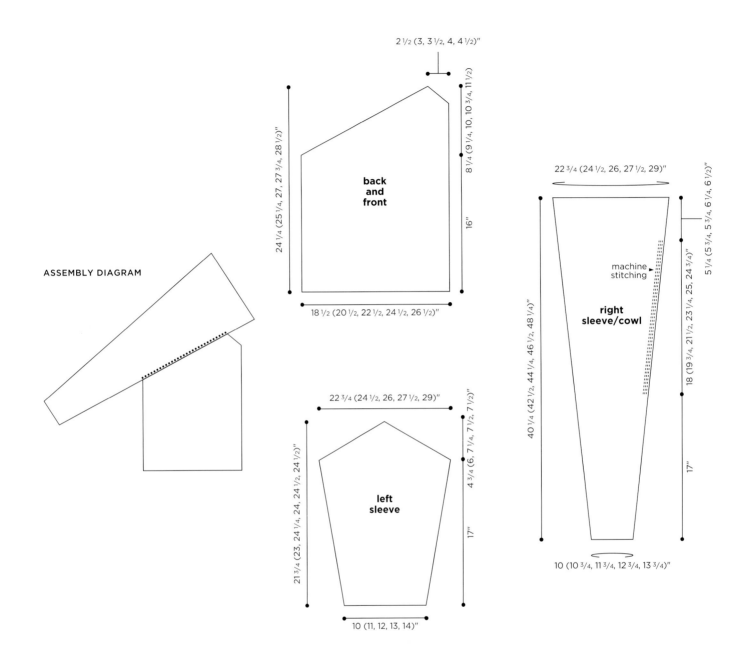

2 1/2 (3, 3 1/2, 4, 4 1/2)"

8 1/4 (9 1/4, 10, 10 3/4, 11 1/2)"

back
and
front

24 1/4 (25 1/4, 27, 27 3/4, 28 1/2)"

16"

18 1/2 (20 1/2, 22 1/2, 24 1/2, 26 1/2)"

ASSEMBLY DIAGRAM

22 3/4 (24 1/2, 26, 27 1/2, 29)"

5 1/4 (5 3/4, 5 3/4, 6 1/4, 6 1/2)"

machine
stitching

right
sleeve/cowl

40 1/4 (42 1/2, 44 1/4, 46 1/2, 48 1/4)"

18 (19 3/4, 21 1/2, 23 1/4, 25, 24 3/4)"

17"

10 (10 3/4, 11 3/4, 12 3/4, 13 3/4)"

22 3/4 (24 1/2, 26, 27 1/2, 29)"

4 3/4 (6, 7 1/4, 7 1/2, 7 1/2)"

left
sleeve

21 3/4 (23, 24 1/4, 24, 24 1/2)"

17"

10 (11, 12, 13, 14)"

Shape Sleeve/Cowl: Continuing in pattern as established, increase 2 sts every 6 rnds as follows: ****Increase Rnd 1:** *K15 (17, 19, 21, 23, 25) sts, yo, k1, yo, ssk, yo, k2tog, k2; repeat from * to last 4 sts, [k2tog] twice.

Work 2 rnds even.

Increase Rnd 2: *K15 (17, 19, 21, 23, 25) sts, yo, k1, yo, ssk, yo*, [k2tog] twice; repeat between *, end k2tog, k2.

Work 2 rnds even.

Repeat from ** until 19 increases have been completed, ending with Increase Rnd 1—61 (65, 69, 73, 77) sts. Work 2 rnds even.

Increase 2 sts every 8 rnds as follows: **Work Increase Rnd 2. Work 3 rnds even. Work Increase Rnd 1. Work 3 rnds even. Repeat from ** until 36 (39, 41, 44, 46) increases have been completed, ending with Increase Rnd 1 (2, 2, 1, 1)—97 (104 110, 117, 123) sts. Work even until piece measures 40 1/4 (42 1/2, 44 1/4, 46 1/2, 48 1/4)" from the beginning. BO all sts. *Note: You may want to leave sts on needles for blocking, since you may have to work additional rows after machine stitching [see Finishing].*

FINISHING

Block all pieces to measurements. Note that Sleeve/Cowl may block slightly larger due to stretchy quality of openwork. Hold left Sleeve and Sleeve/Cowl up to each other (do not lay down) and pm for underarm on Sleeve/Cowl. Now lay Sleeve/Cowl down and pm 18 (19 3/4, 21 1/2, 23 1/4, 24 3/4)" above underarm marker. Hand baste a line along fold on underarm side between markers. Using sewing machine and very small sts, sew three rows, closely spaced, on each side of basting thread, and at each end of the three rows, to secure sts. Machine stitching will pull knitted fabric differently depending on size of sewn sts and tension of machine. Compare length of sewn rows to opening on front of sweater and extend length of sewn portion if necessary to fit opening. There should still be 5 1/4 (5 3/4, 5 3/4, 6 1/4, 6 1/2)" of Sleeve/Cowl above opening. If not, continue Sleeve/Cowl piece until it measures 5 1/4 (5 3/4, 5 3/4, 6 1/4, 6 1/2)" above opening. Cut down center of machine stitching and sew Sleeve/Cowl to Front and Back. Sew left shoulder. Sew in left Sleeve. Sew side and Sleeve seams.

Cabled Spiral Pullover

I think of this cable pattern as the art deco version of a seashell. The curves have been squared off, and rounded angles replace sinuous lines. Although stylized, the outline of a shell remains, growing from a point to accommodate the growing animal within. When designing this pullover, I chose ease of knitting over geometric accuracy, limiting myself to two-over-two cables. The decreases that shape the yoke and coincide with the narrowing of the seashell shape are placed in the reverse Stockinette-stitch sections on either side of the shell motifs, so they don't interfere with the cable.

NOTES

❱ Back, Front and Sleeves are worked back and forth to underarm, then joined at the Yoke and worked in the rnd.

BACK

Using smaller needles, CO 96 (106, 116, 126, 136) sts; knit 2 rows. (RS) Change to larger needles and St st. Work even until piece measures 16" from the beginning, ending with a WS row. (RS) BO 5 (6, 7, 8, 9) sts at beginning of next 2 rows—86 (94, 102, 110, 118) sts remain. Place sts on holder for Yoke Base.

FRONT

Work as for Back until piece measures 14½" from the beginning, ending with a WS row.

Shape Yoke Base: (RS) Work 11 (12, 13, 14, 15) sts, join a second ball of yarn, work 74 (82, 90, 98, 106) sts and place on holder for Yoke. Work across remaining 11 (12, 13, 14, 15) sts. Working BOTH SIDES AT SAME TIME, work 1 row even. (RS) Decrease 1 st at each neck edge every other row 6 times as follows: Work to last 3 sts of left side, ssk, k1; on right side, k1, k2tog, work to end—5 (6, 7, 8, 9) sts remain each side for underarm. Work 1 (WS) row even. (RS) BO all sts.

SLEEVES (make 2)

Using smaller needles, CO 47 (50, 53, 56, 59) sts; knit 2 rows. (RS) Change to larger needles and St st. Work even for 1½ (2, 1½, 1, ½)", ending with a WS row.

Shape Sleeves: (RS) Increase 1 st each side every 8 rows 0 (0, 1, 5, 8) times, every 10 rows 0 (10, 10, 7, 5) times, then every 12 rows 9 (0, 0, 0, 0) times as follows: K2, m1, knit to last 2 sts, m1, k2—65 (70, 75, 80, 85) sts. Work even until piece measures 17" from the beginning, ending with a WS row.

Shape Yoke Base: (RS) BO 5 (6, 7, 8, 9) sts at beginning of next 2 rows—55 (58, 61, 64, 67) sts remain for Yoke Base. Transfer sts to holder for Yoke.

SIZES
Petite (Small, Medium, Large, X-Large)
Shown in size Small

FINISHED MEASUREMENTS
36 (40, 44, 48, 52)" chest

YARN
Jaeger Extra Fine Merino DK (100% extra-fine merino wool; 136 yards/50 grams): 13 (14, 16, 18, 20) balls #940 ocean

NEEDLES
One pair straight needles size US 5 (3.75 mm)
One pair straight needles size US 6 (4 mm)
One 24" (60 cm) circular (circ) needle size US 6 (4 mm)
One 16" (40 cm) circular needle size US 6 (4 mm)
One 16" (40 cm) circular needle size US 5 (3.75 mm)

NOTIONS
Stitch holders; stitch marker

GAUGE
21 sts and 28 rows = 4" (10 cm) in Stockinette stitch (St st) using larger needles

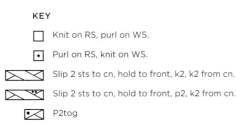

KEY

- ☐ Knit on RS, purl on WS.
- ⊡ Purl on RS, knit on WS.
- ⧄ Slip 2 sts to cn, hold to front, k2, k2 from cn.
- ⧄ Slip 2 sts to cn, hold to front, p2, k2 from cn.
- ⧄ P2tog

☐ Repeat for Neckband

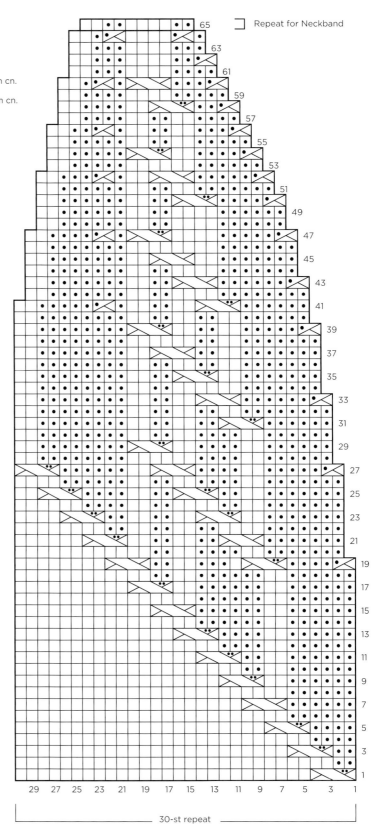

30-st repeat

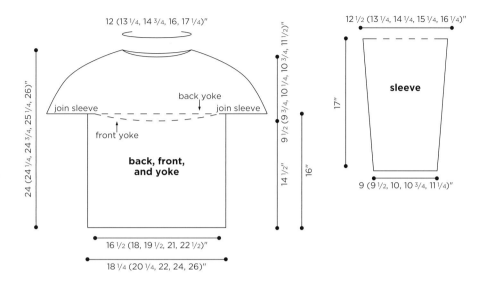

12 (13 1/4, 14 3/4, 16, 17 1/4)"

12 1/2 (13 1/4, 14 1/4, 15 1/4, 16 1/4)"

24 (24 1/4, 24 3/4, 25 1/4, 26)"

9 1/2 (9 3/4, 10 1/4, 10 3/4, 11 1/2)"

14 1/2"

16"

17"

sleeve

9 (9 1/2, 10, 10 3/4, 11 1/4)"

back yoke

join sleeve

join sleeve

front yoke

back, front, and yoke

16 1/2 (18, 19 1/2, 21, 22 1/2)"

18 1/4 (20 1/4, 22, 24, 26)"

YOKE

Sew side and Sleeve seams. Using larger circ needle, beginning at Back, work across 86 (94, 102, 110, 118) sts from Back Yoke Base, then 55 (58, 61, 64, 67) sts from left Sleeve holder, pick up and knit 8 sts along left Front shaping edge, work across 74 (82, 90, 98, 106) sts from Front holder, pick up and knit 8 sts along right Front shaping edge, work across 55 (58, 61, 64, 67) sts from right Sleeve holder—286 (308, 330, 352, 374) sts. Join for working in the rnd, being careful not to twist sts; pm for beginning of rnd. Working in St st, decrease (decrease, decrease, increase, increase) 16 (8, 0, 8, 16) sts on first rnd—270 (300, 330, 360, 390) sts. Work even for 2 (4, 8, 12, 16) rnds. Begin Cable Pattern from Chart, working decreases as indicated—108 (120, 132, 144, 156) sts remain after Chart is complete. *Neckband:* Change to smaller circ needle and continue in pattern as indicated on Row 65 of Chart for 8". BO all sts. Sew underarms.

Shell Tank

As with the Cabled Spiral Pullover in this chapter, the concept of the seashell has been highly stylized in this piece. I exaggerated the angularity by increasing the size of the shell in a very predictable manner. The conical shape formed by the cable panel provides a great point for an asymmetrical hem. I built the rest of the front around it. To keep the directions for shaping easy to follow, I worked the front in three pieces: the wide right front panel, a narrower left front panel, and the wedge-shaped cable panel in between. A gentle flare at the sides, the visual distraction of the pointed hem, and the diagonal line across the chest all add up to a very flattering garment.

NOTES

❱ *Stitch Pattern:* see left.

❱ Front is made in 3 separate pieces, then sewn together.

BACK

Using smaller needles, CO 114 (122, 134, 142) sts; begin 2×2 Rib. Work even for 1″, ending with a WS row. (RS) Change to larger needles and St st, knit 1 row, decrease 8 (6, 8, 6) sts across row—106 (116, 126, 136) sts remain. Work even for 1″, ending with a WS row.

Shape Back: (RS) Decrease 1 st each side every 12 rows 5 times as follows: K3, k2tog, work to last 5 sts, ssk, k3—96 (106, 116, 126) sts remain. Work even until piece measures 11″ from the beginning, ending with a WS row.

Shape Armholes: (RS) BO 4 sts at beginning of next 2 (2, 2, 4) rows, 3 sts at beginning of next 2 (4, 4, 4) rows, 2 sts at beginning of next 4 (2, 6, 4) rows, then decrease 1 st each side every other row 2 (3, 2, 2) times as follows: K3, k2tog, work to last 5 sts, ssk, k3—70 (76, 80, 86) sts remain. Work even until piece measures 16 ½ (17, 17 ½, 18)" from the beginning, ending with a WS row.

Shape Neck: (RS) Work 24 (27, 29, 32) sts; join a second ball of yarn and BO center 22 sts, work to end. Working BOTH SIDES AT SAME TIME, BO 5 sts at each neck edge twice—14 (17, 19, 22) sts remain each side for shoulders. Work even until armhole measures 6 ½ (7, 7 ½, 8)", ending with a WS row. BO all sts.

LEFT FRONT

Using larger needles CO 21 (25, 33, 37) sts; begin 2×2 Rib as follows:

Row 1 (RS): *K2, p2; repeat from * to last st, k1.

Row 2: P1, *k2, p2; repeat from * to end.

Work even as established for 1″, ending with a WS row. (RS) Change to larger needles and St st, knit 1 row, decrease 1 (0, 3, 2) sts across row—20 (25, 30, 35) sts remain. Work 1 row even.

Shape Back: (RS) Decrease 1 st every 12 rows 5 times as follows: K3, k2tog, work to end—15 (20, 25, 30) sts remain. Work even until piece measures 11″ from the beginning, ending with a WS row.

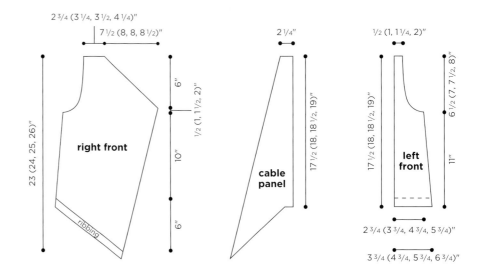

Shape Armhole

Shape Armhole: (RS) BO 4 sts at beginning of row every other row 1 (1, 1, 2) times, 3 sts 1 (2, 2, 2) times, 2 sts 2 (1, 3, 2) times, then decrease 1 st every other row 2 (3, 2, 2) times as follows: K3, k2tog, work to end—2 (5, 7, 10) sts remain. Work even until piece measures same as for Back to shoulder. BO all sts.

CENTER FRONT CABLE PANEL

Using larger needles, CO 13 sts; begin Cable pattern from Chart. Complete entire Chart, working increases and decreases as indicated—20 sts remain. Work even as established until piece measures same as for Back to shoulder, measured along shorter edge. BO all sts.

RIGHT FRONT

Note: Ribbing along bottom of Right Front will be picked up and worked after piece is completed.

Using larger needles, CO 3 sts; begin St st, work 1 (WS) row even.

Shape Right Front: *NOTE: When shaping this piece, left edge is shaped on WS rows and right edge is shaped on RS rows. All WS row shaping is given first, then all RS row shaping is given. Edges must be shaped simultaneously; read through all shaping instructions carefully before beginning.*

(WS) Continuing in St st as established, work WS rows as follows: CO 2 sts at beginning of row every WS row 20 (14, 10, 4) times, then 3 sts 0 (6, 10, 16) times; work even for 6 WS rows. Decrease 1 st every 6 WS rows 5 times as follows: P3, ssp, work to end; then work even on WS rows until piece measures same as for Back to armhole shaping, **Shape Armhole:** BO 4 sts at beginning of row every WS row 1 (1, 1, 2) times, 3 sts 1 (2, 2, 2) times, 2 sts 2 (1, 3, 2) times, then decrease 1 st every WS row 2 (3, 2, 2) times as follows: P3, ssp, work to end, and AT THE SAME TIME, work RS rows as follows: Increase 1 st every other RS row 29 (30, 31, 32) times as follows: K3, m1, work to end; then work even on RS rows until piece measures ½ (1, 1½, 2)" from beginning of armhole shaping.

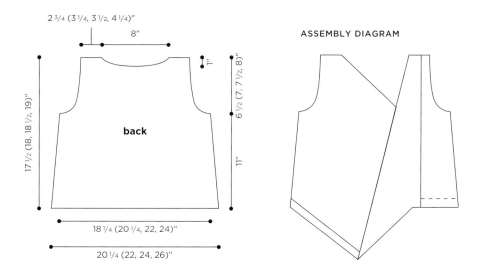

2 3/4 (3 1/4, 3 1/2, 4 1/4)"

8"

1"

6 1/2 (7, 7 1/2, 8)"

11"

17 1/2 (18, 18 1/2, 19)"

back

18 1/4 (20 1/4, 22, 24)"

20 1/4 (22, 24, 26)"

ASSEMBLY DIAGRAM

Shape Neck: (RS) Continuing WS row shaping above, BO 3 sts at beginning of every RS row 0 (2, 2, 4) times, then 2 sts 20 (18, 18, 16) times—14 (17, 19, 22) sts remain. Work 1 WS row even. BO all sts.

Ribbing: Using smaller needles, pick up and knit 49 (57, 61, 69) sts along shaping edge, from left edge to first CO sts. (WS) Begin 2×2 Rib as follows: *P2, k2; repeat from * to last st, p1. Work even for 1". BO all sts in Rib.

FINISHING

Sew right shoulder seam. *Neckband:* Using smaller needles, beginning at Right Front, pick up and knit 98 (102, 102, 104) sts around neck shaping on Right Front and Back. Knit 1 row. Purl 1 row. Knit 1 row. BO all sts purlwise. Sew left shoulder seam. *Armhole Edging:* Using smaller needles, pick up and knit 88 (94, 100, 106) sts around armhole edge. Work as for Neckband. Sew Center Front Cable Panel to Right and Left Fronts [see assembly diagram]. Sew side seams.

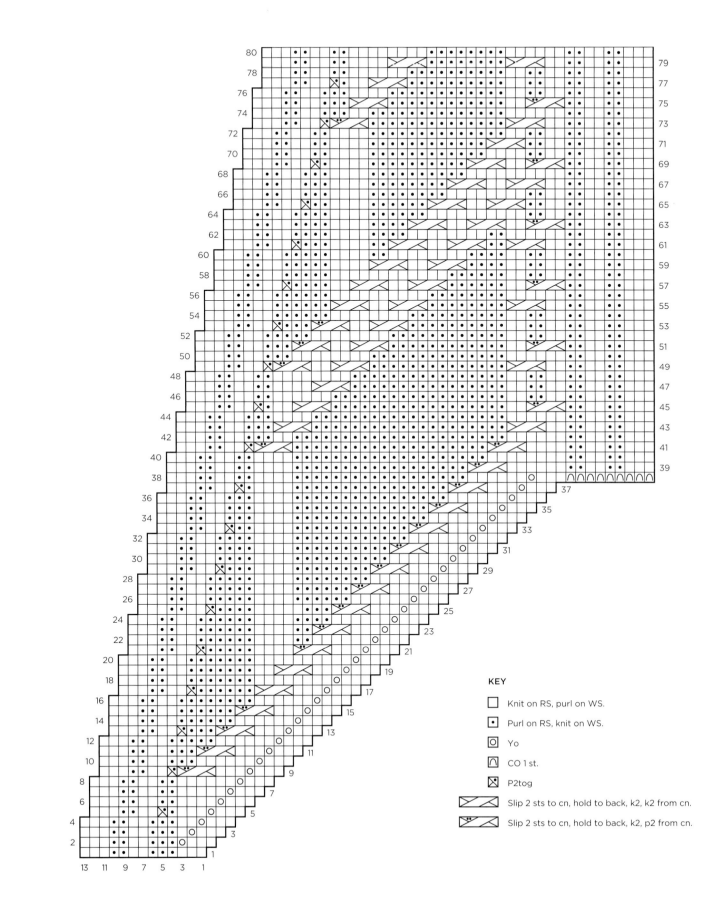

KEY

☐ Knit on RS, purl on WS.

• Purl on RS, knit on WS.

⊙ Yo

∩ CO 1 st.

⊠ P2tog

▱ Slip 2 sts to cn, hold to back, k2, k2 from cn.

▱ Slip 2 sts to cn, hold to back, k2, p2 from cn.

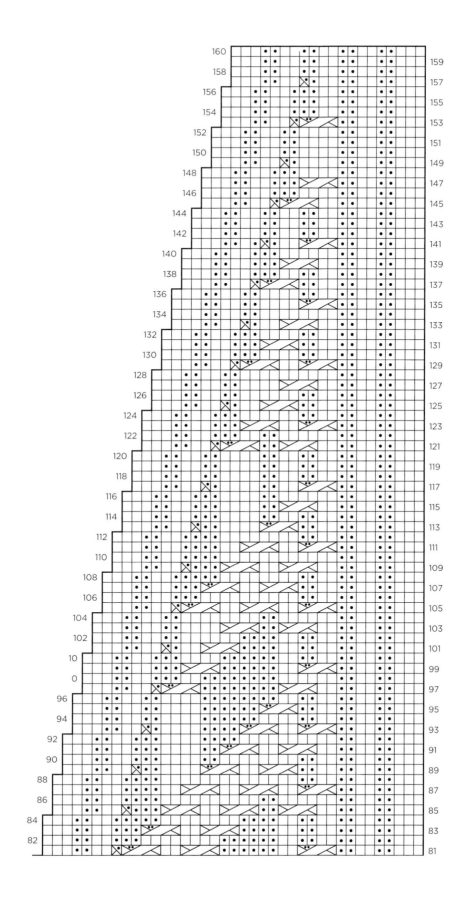

Ram's Horn Jacket

Rams' horns are usually gently curving logarithmic spirals. As the animal grows, the growth end of the horn—closest to the head—becomes larger as keratin is added in an increasingly larger diameter. The keratin is not added in even amounts at all points at the base of the horn, however. Growth is a bit slower toward one side of the horn, so it grows in a curve rather than straight out. So curves the collar on this jacket, which is knit back and forth on straight needles and sewn together. To simulate the shaping of a ram's horn, increases are worked at a constant rate at each end while the spiral shape is achieved with short rows. The jacket body—to which the collar is sewn—is a basic swing shape with hemmed edgings.

NOTES

▶ *Stitch Pattern:* see right.

BACK

Using medium (size US 6) needles, CO 106 (116, 126, 136, 146) sts; begin St st. Work even for 3″, ending with a RS row. (WS) Knit 1 row (turning row). (RS) Change to largest (size US 7) needles and St st and work even for 3″, ending with a WS row.

Shape Back: (RS) Decrease 1 st each side every 10 rows 5 times as follows: K2, k2tog, work to last 4 sts, ssk, k2—96 (106, 116, 126, 136) sts remain. Work even until piece measures 11 1/2″ from turning row, ending with a WS row.

Shape Armholes: (RS) BO 4 sts at beginning of next 0 (0, 0, 2, 2) rows, 3 sts at beginning of next 2 (2, 4, 4, 6) rows, 2 sts at beginning of next 4 (6, 6, 4, 4) rows, then decrease 1 st each side every other row 3 times—72 (82, 86, 92, 96) sts remain. Work even until piece measures 8 (8 1/2, 9, 9 1/2, 10)″ from beginning of armhole shaping, ending with a WS row.

Shape Shoulders and Neck: (RS) BO 7 (7, 8, 8, 9) sts, work 24 (26, 26, 28, 28) sts; join a second ball of yarn and BO center 14 (16, 18, 20, 22) sts, work to end. Working BOTH SIDES AT SAME TIME, BO 7 (7, 8, 8, 9) sts at beginning of next row, then 7 (8, 8, 9, 9) sts at beginning of next 4 rows and AT THE SAME TIME, BO 5 sts at each neck edge twice.

RIGHT FRONT

Using medium (size US 6) needles, CO 53 (58, 63, 68, 73) sts; begin St st. Work even for 3″, ending with a RS row. (WS) Knit 1 row (turning row). (RS) Change to largest (size US 7) needles and St st and work even for 3″.

Shape Right Front: (RS) Decrease 1 st at end of row every 10 rows 5 times as follows: Work to last 4 sts, ssk, k2—48 (53, 58, 63, 68) sts remain. Work even until piece measures 11 1/2″ from turning row, ending with a RS row.

Shape Armholes: (WS) BO 4 sts at beginning of row every other row 0 (0, 0, 1, 1) times, 3 sts 1 (1, 2, 2, 3) times, 2 sts 2 (3, 3, 2, 2) times, then 1 st 3 times—38 (41, 43, 46, 48) sts remain. Work even until piece measures 15 (15 1/2, 16, 16 1/2, 17)″ from turning row, ending with a WS row.

Shape Neck: (RS) BO 5 sts at beginning of row every other row 0 (0, 0, 0, 1) time, 4 sts 0 (0, 0, 1, 0) time, 3 sts 1 (2, 2, 1, 1) times, 2 sts 2 (1, 1, 1, 1) times, then 1 st 10 (10, 11, 11, 11) times—21 (23, 24, 26, 27) sts remain, and AT THE SAME TIME, when piece measures same as for Back to shoulder, ending with a WS row, Shape shoulder as for Back.

SIZES
Petite (Small, Medium, Large, X-Large)
Shown in size Petite

FINISHED MEASUREMENTS
38 1/2 (42 1/2, 46 1/2, 50 1/2, 54 1/2)″ chest

YARN
Classic Elite Yarns Renaissance (100% wool; 112 yards/50 grams): 14 (15, 16, 18, 20) hanks #7173 Tuscan field

NEEDLES
One pair straight needles size US 5 (3.75 mm)
One pair straight needles size US 6 (4 mm)
One pair straight needles size US 7 (4.5 mm)
Change needle size if necessary to obtain correct gauge.

NOTIONS
Stitch markers; shawl pin (One World Button Supply Co.)

GAUGE
20 sts and 26 rows = 4″ (10 cm) in Stockinette st (St st) using largest (size US 7) needles

STITCH PATTERN
Openwork Stitch:
(multiple of 14 sts; 1-row repeat)
All Rows: [Yo, p2tog] 7 times.

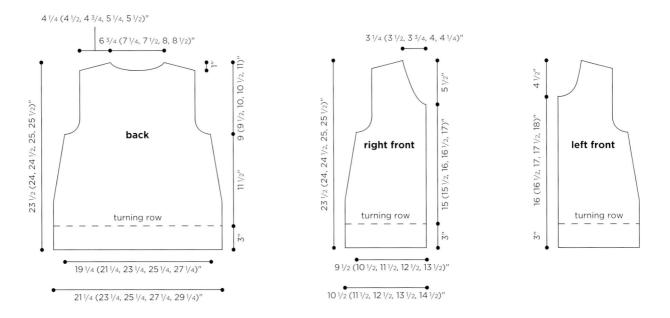

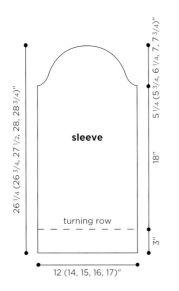

LEFT FRONT

Work as for Right Front, reversing all shaping, to beginning of neck shaping—38 (41, 43, 46, 48) sts remain. Work 1 row even.

Shape Neck: (WS) BO 4 sts at beginning of row every other row once, 3 sts once, 2 sts 3 times, then 1 st 0 (1, 2, 3, 4) times—20 (22, 23, 25, 26) sts remain, and, AT THE SAME TIME, when piece measures same as for Back to shoulder, Shape shoulder as for Back.

SLEEVES (make 2)

Using medium (size US 6) needles, CO 65 (70, 75, 80, 85) sts; begin St st. Work even for 3", ending with a RS row. (WS) Knit 1 row (turning row). (RS) Change to largest (size US 7) needles and St st and work even until piece measures 18" from turning row, ending with a WS row.

Shape Cap: (RS) BO 3 sts at beginning of next 2 rows, 2 sts at beginning of next 2 rows, then decrease 1 st each side every other row 13 (15, 17, 19, 21) times as follows: K2, k2tog, work to last 4 sts, ssk, k2—29 (30, 31, 32, 33) sts remain. BO 2 sts at beginning of next 2 rows, then 3 sts at beginning of next 2 rows—19 (20, 21, 22, 23) sts remain. BO all sts.

LEFT FRONT BAND

Using smallest (size US 5) needles, CO 21 sts.

Establish Pattern:

Row 1 (RS): K2, *p1, k1; repeat from * to last st, k1.

Row 2: *K1, p1; repeat from * to last st, k1.

Repeat Rows 1 and 2 for Pattern.

Work even as established until piece measures 16 (16 1/2, 17, 17 1/2, 18)" from the beginning, ending with a WS row. BO all sts.

RIGHT FRONT BAND

Work as for Left Front Band until piece measures 14 (14 1/2, 15, 15 1/2, 16)" from the beginning, ending with a WS row. (RS) BO 4 sts at beginning of row every other row 4 times—5 sts remain. Work 1 row even. (RS) BO all sts.

COLLAR

Using largest (size US 7) needles, CO 4 sts.

Establish Pattern:

Rows 1 and 3 (RS): K1, yo, p2tog, k1.

Rows 2 and 4: P1, yo, p2tog, p1.

Row 5: K1, m1, yo, p2tog, m1, k1—6 sts.

Rows 6 and 8: P2, yo, p2tog, p2.

Row 7: K2, yo, p2tog, k2.

Row 9: K1, m1, k1, yo, p2tog, k1, m1, k1—8 sts.

Rows 10 and 12: P1, [yo, p2tog] 3 times, p1.

Row 11: K1, [yo, p2tog] 3 times, p1.

Row 13: K1, m1, [yo, p2tog] 3 times, m1, k1—10 sts.

Rows 14 and 16: P2, [yo, p2tog] 3 times, p2.

Row 15: K2, [yo, p2tog] 3 times, k2.

Row 17: K1, m1, k1, [yo, p2tog] 3 times, k1, m1, k1—12 sts.

Rows 18 and 20: P1, [yo, p2tog] 5 times, p1.

Row 19: K1, [yo, p2tog] 5 times, p1.

Row 21: K1, m1, [yo, p2tog] 5 times, m1, k1—14 sts.

Rows 22 and 25: P2, [yo, p2tog] 5 times, p2.

Row 23: K2, [yo, p2tog] 5 times, k2.

Row 25: K1, m1, k1, [yo, p2tog] 5 times, k1, m1, k1—16 sts.

Row 26: P1, place marker (pm), [yo, p2tog] 7 times, pm, p1.

Continue shaping Collar, increasing 1 st at each end every 4 rows as established, working increased sts in St st, and working Openwork Stitch between markers. Work even until you have 26 sts, ending with a WS row.

Continuing to work Openwork Stitch between markers, work short row shaping as follows:

Row 1 (RS): K1, m1, work to 2 sts after second marker, turn.

Row 2: Yo, work to 2 sts after second marker, turn.

Row 3: Yo, work to yo after second marker, k2tog [yo and next st], work to last st, m1, k1.

Row 4: Work to yo after second marker, ssp [yo and next st], work to end.

Row 5: K1, m1, work to 1 st after st made by k2tog of previous RS row, k1, turn.

Row 6: Yo, work to 1 st after st made by ssp of previous WS row, p1, turn.

Row 7: Yo, work to yo after second marker, k2tog [yo and next st], work to last st, m1, k1.

Row 8: Work to yo after second marker, ssp [yo and next st], work to end.

*Repeat Rows 5–8 until there are only 2 sts left on the left-hand needle after working the ssp on Row 8. Repeat Rows 1–4 once. Repeat from * until 39 sts have been increased each side, ending with a WS row—94 sts. (RS) Knit 2 rows. Purl 1 row. Knit 1 row. BO all sts purlwise. Fold collar in half so WS's face each other; sew to neckline, easing collar to fit.

FINISHING

Sew shoulder seams. Set in Sleeves. Sew side and Sleeve seams. Sew Front Bands to Fronts.

Chapter 4

PHYLLOTAXIS*

* *phyllotaxis: (n) the principles governing leaf arrangement*

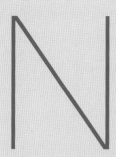No one knows for certain, but scientists believe there are over 260,000 species of plants. These diverse species range from tiny, barely visible plants growing on the forest floor to the largest living things—like the sequoia trees of California, which tower over us by as much as 280 feet. Yet there are only three basic patterns that describe all plants on earth, from the tropical rain forests of Brazil to the taiga in Siberia. The most common of the three arrangements, phyllotaxis, describes 80 percent of plant species, and is, I think, the most fascinating. In this arrangement, leaves grow in double spirals (traveling clockwise and counterclockwise) around a stem. The angle between one leaf and the next averages, 137½°. This is not an arbitrary angle. The Greeks referred to it as "the golden angle" and it's the angle associated with the Fibonacci series (see page 41). If you count the number of spirals turning in each direction, you'll find that the two numbers (the number of spirals traveling clockwise and the number of spirals traveling counterclockwise) represent a pair of sequential numbers from the Fibonacci series. The Fibonacci series is 0, 1, 1, 2, 3, 5, 8, 13, 21, 34, etc. For instance: the leaf spirals may occur 8 times clockwise and 13 times counterclockwise, or 21 times clockwise and 34 times counterclockwise, etc. To easily view the double spirals of phyllotaxis, look closely at sunflowers, pinecones, and pineapples. Perhaps this is the most efficient way for new growth buds to pack together in the growing tip of the plant (not unlike the efficient packing of bubbles into rafts of hexagons and clusters of pentagons).

I was true to the mathematical concept of phyllotaxis when designing the Diamond Tunic (page 100) and the Phyllotaxis Scarf (page 112), though I did not reference any plant in particular. The double spirals on the Sunflower Tam (page 114) and the Phyllo Yoked Pullover (page 104) look like flower heads, although I modified the mathematics in order to simplify the knitting (and designing). For a completely different approach to the subject, I arranged leaves in a spiral to create the body for the Roundabout Leaf Tank (page 108); again, I took great liberties with the math but remained true to nature's original patterns.

Diamond Tunic

As the idea for this book was gelling in my mind, I combed bookstores and Web sites for inspirational images of nature's patterns and understandable explanations of the science behind them. While I was reading up on phyllotaxis, I came upon On Growth and Form *by D'Arcy Wentworth Thompson. In this early classic about patterns in nature, Thompson illustrates the mathematical proportion of the double spirals with a simplified diagram of spirals projected onto a flat surface. Seen from this perspective, the spirals become straight lines.*

I based the diamond pattern on this pullover on one of Thompson's simplified diagrams, allowing two lines to slant in one direction for every one in the opposing direction. I decided to mirror the pattern on either side of a center line, which makes some interesting shapes where they meet. No doubt, a more "predictable" diamond pattern would be easier to knit, but I couldn't resist the nerdy temptation to mimic phyllotaxis accurately. The shift in the diamonds is more interesting for the additional effort.

SIZES
Petite (Small, Medium, Large, X-Large)
Shown in size Small

FINISHED MEASUREMENTS
To fit bust 32-34 (36-38, 40-42, 44-46, 48-50)"; 41 (45, 49, 52 1/2, 56 1/2)" chest

YARN
Goddess Yarns Hayden (85% pima cotton/15% silk; 90 yards/50 grams): 12 (13, 14, 16, 18) balls #3568 pumpkin

NEEDLES
One pair straight needles size US 6 (4 mm)
One pair straight needles size US 7 (4.5 mm)
Change needle size if necessary to obtain correct gauge.

GAUGE
21 sts and 28 rows = 4" (10 cm) in Diamond Pattern from Chart using larger needles

STITCH PATTERN
Garter Stitch:
(any number of sts; 1-row repeat)
Knit all rows.

NOTES

▶ *Stitch Pattern:* see left.

BACK

Using smaller needles, CO 108 (118, 128, 138, 148) sts; begin Garter St (knit all sts in all rows). Work even for 5 rows. Change to larger needles and purl 1 row. (RS) Begin Diamond Pattern from Chart as indicated for your size, work Section A 2 (2, 3, 3, 3) times, then Section B 2 (2, 3, 3, 3) times, work to end as indicated for your size. Work even until piece measures 18 1/2", ending with a WS row.

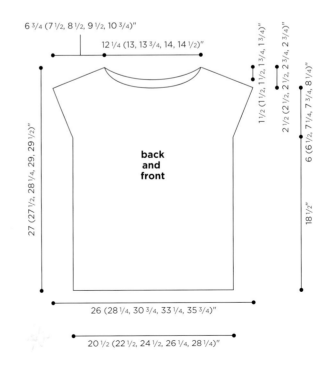

6 3/4 (7 1/2, 8 1/2, 9 1/2, 10 3/4)"

12 1/4 (13, 13 3/4, 14, 14 1/2)"

1 1/2 (1 1/2, 1 1/2, 1 3/4, 1 3/4)"

2 1/2 (2 1/2, 2, 2 3/4, 2 3/4)"

6 (6 1/2, 7 1/4, 7 3/4, 8 1/4)"

27 (27 1/2, 28 1/4, 29, 29 1/2)"

back and front

18 1/2"

26 (28 1/4, 30 3/4, 33 1/4, 35 3/4)"

20 1/2 (22 1/2, 24 1/2, 26 1/4, 28 1/4)"

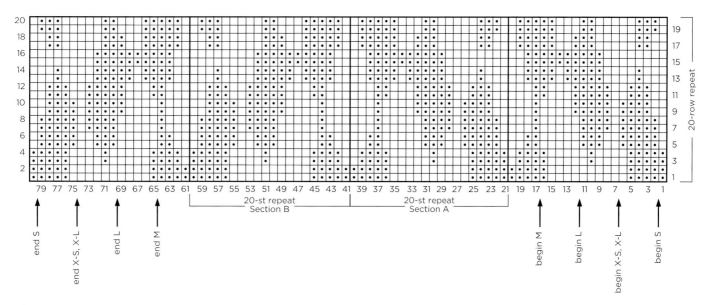

Shape Cap Sleeves: (RS) Increase 1 st each side every other row 7 (7, 9, 9, 11) times, then every 4 rows 7 (8, 8, 9, 9) times as follows, working increased sts in Diamond Pattern. *NOTE: As you increase sts at either edge, you will eventually reach the last st in the chart. To continue the Diamond Pattern past the last st, start back at st #20 for the right edge and st #61 for the left edge, and work out to either end of the chart until you complete the increases.* K1, m1, work to last st, m1, k1—136 (148, 162, 174, 188) sts. Work even until piece measures 6 (6 1/2, 7 1/4, 7 3/4, 8 1/4)" from beginning of armhole shaping, ending with a WS row.

Shape Shoulders and Neck: (RS) BO 4 (4, 5, 5, 5) sts at beginning of next 8 rows. (RS) BO 4 (4, 5, 5, 6) sts, work 52 (56, 60, 65, 71) sts; join a second ball of yarn and BO center 24 (28, 32, 34, 36) sts, work to end. Working BOTH SIDES AT SAME TIME, BO 4 (4, 5, 5, 6) sts at beginning of next row, then 4 (5, 5, 5, 6) sts at beginning of next 8 (8, 8, 10, 10) rows, and AT THE SAME TIME, BO 5 sts at each neck edge 4 times.

FRONT

Work as for Back to shoulder shaping.

Shape Shoulders and Neck: (RS) BO 4 (4, 5, 5, 6) sts, work 52 (56, 60, 65, 71) sts; join a second ball of yarn and BO center 24 (28, 32, 34, 36) sts, work to end. Working BOTH SIDES AT SAME TIME, BO 4 (4, 5, 5, 6) sts at beginning of next 17 (9, 17, 19, 7) rows, then 0 (5, 0, 0, 6) sts at beginning of next 0 (8, 0, 0, 12) rows, and AT THE SAME TIME, BO 4 sts at each neck edge once, 3 sts twice, then 2 sts 5 (5, 5, 6, 6) times.

FINISHING

Sew left shoulder seam. **Neckband:** Using smaller needles, beginning at right neck edge, pick up and knit 120 (130, 140, 150, 160) sts around neck shaping. Knit 2 rows. BO all sts knitwise. Sew right shoulder seam. **Armhole Edging:** Using smaller needles, pick up and knit 60 (65, 69, 74, 78) sts around armhole edge. Knit 2 rows. BO all sts knitwise. Sew side seams.

KEY

☐ Knit on RS, purl on WS.

⊡ Purl on RS, knit on WS.

Phyllo Yoked Pullover

I worked with the concept of phyllotaxis to create the pretty yoke pattern for this basic pullover but decided not to be a purist about the science. There are two spirals traveling in opposing directions, very much like spirals on a sunflower or a pinecone. That much rings true. But my spirals interlace and occur with equal frequency, which is not how phyllotaxis works in nature. The counterclockwise spirals are made with twisted stitches, and the clockwise spirals are made with lace eyelet and decrease combinations. The yoke is shaped by working decrease rounds periodically between pattern rows, and the decreases are an integral part of the pattern.

NOTES

▶ Back, Front, and Sleeves are knit back and forth to underarm, then Yoke is knit in-the-rnd.

BACK

CO 96 (106, 116, 126, 136) sts; begin St st. Work even until piece measures 16″ from the beginning, ending with a WS row. (RS) BO 5 (6, 7, 8, 9) sts at beginning of next 2 rows. Place remaining 86 (94, 102, 110, 118) sts on holder for Yoke.

FRONT

Work as for Back until piece measures 14½″ from the beginning, ending with a WS row.

Shape Front: (RS) Continuing in St st, work 11 (12, 13, 14, 15) sts, place marker (pm); join a second ball of yarn, work 74 (82, 90, 98, 106) sts and place on holder for Yoke, work to end. Working BOTH SIDES AT SAME TIME, work 1 row even. (RS) Decrease 1 st each side of Yoke this row, then every other row 5 times as follows: On right side of Yoke sts, work to 4 sts before marker, ssk, k2; on left side of Yoke sts, k2, k2tog, work to end—5 (6, 7, 8, 9) sts remain each side. BO remaining sts.

SIZES
X-Small (Small, Medium, Large, X-Large)
Shown in size Small

FINISHED MEASUREMENTS
36½ (40½, 44, 48, 51½)″ chest

YARN
Rowan Calmer (75% cotton/25% microfiber; 175 yards/50 grams): 7 (8, 9, 10, 11) balls #476 coral

NEEDLES
One pair straight needles size US 7 (4.5 mm)
One 24″ (60 cm) circular (circ) needle size US 7 (4.5 mm)
One 16″ (40 cm) circular needle size US 7 (4.5 mm)
One 16″ (40 cm) circular needle size US 5 (3.75 mm)
Change needle size if necessary to obtain correct gauge.

NOTIONS
Stitch holders (4), stitch marker

GAUGE
21 sts and 28 rows = 4″ (10 cm) in Stockinette stitch (St st) using larger needles

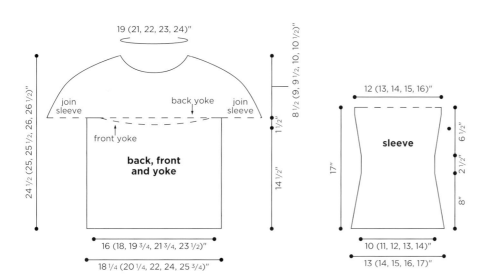

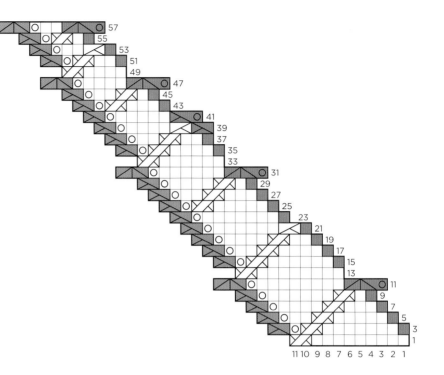

KEY

☐ Knit

▣ Knit on first repeat only; on remaining repeats, it will be knit together with last st from previous repeat.

◹ K2tog, but do not drop sts from left-hand needle, insert right-hand needle between 2 sts just worked and knit first st again, slip both sts from left-hand needle together.

◙ Yo

◺ K2tog

◤ Ssk (last st of repeat with first st of following repeat).

◣ Ssk (last st of last repeat with first st of first repeat).

◣◙ Yo, ssk (last st of last repeat with first st of first repeat).

◣◙ Yo, k3tog (last st of last repeat with first 2 sts of first repeat).

◺ K3tog (last st of repeat with first 2 sts of following repeat).

SLEEVES

CO 69 (74, 79, 84, 89) sts; begin St st. Work even for 2″, ending with a WS row.

Shape Sleeve: (RS) Decrease 1 st each side this row, then every 6 rows 7 times as follows: K2, k2tog, work to last 4 sts, ssk, k2—53 (58, 63, 68, 73) sts remain. Work even until piece measures 10 ½″ from the beginning, ending with a WS row. (RS) Increase 1 st each side this row, then every 8 rows 5 times as follows: K2, m1, work to last 2 sts, m1, k2—65 (70, 75, 80, 85) sts. Work even until piece measures 17″ from the beginning, ending with a WS row. (RS) BO 5 (6, 7, 8, 9) sts at beginning of next 2 rows. Place remaining 55 (58, 61, 64, 67) sts on holder for Yoke.

YOKE

NOTE: Change to 16″ circ needle when work no longer fits on 24″ circ needle.

Sew side and Sleeve seams. Using yarn attached to Back and 24″ circ needle, knit across 84 (94, 102, 110, 118) sts of Back, and 55 (58, 61, 64, 67) sts from left Sleeve holder, pick up and knit 8 sts along Left Front shaping, knit across 74 (82, 90, 98, 106) sts from Front holder, pick up and knit 8 sts along Right Front shaping, knit across 55 (58, 61, 64, 67) sts from right Sleeve holder, pm for beginning of rnd—286 (308, 330, 352, 374) sts. Continuing in St st, work even for 2 (4, 8, 12, 16) rnds. Begin Lace Chart. Work entire Chart once, working decreases as indicated in Chart—104 (112, 120, 128, 136) sts remain. Change to smaller circ needle. Purl 1 rnd. Knit 1 rnd. BO all sts purl-wise. Sew underarm seams.

Roundabout Leaf Tank

This sweater is made out of a spiraling strip, in the same way that leaves grow on a stem. The real design challenge came in keeping the shape simple enough to be able to make it in multiple sizes. I really liked the idea of the asymmetrically pointed bottom edge, so I let the start of my long rectangular strip dangle in front, while tapering the last bit to form a straight edge across the bust at the underarm, where a straight piece is knitted on to complete the sleeves and yoke. The leaves are not placed at 137½° angles to each other, as would be correct in nature; if they were, there would only be about 2½ leaves per rotation, which didn't seem like enough to me even in the petite size. In deference to the original inspiration, I purposefully placed the leaves so that they would stagger in a way similar to natural leaves on a stem. I think it's fun to knit the strip together as you go so there is no tedious sewing afterward. The intentionally-raised line made in the process further defines the spiral. No need to be subtle.

SIZES
Petite (Small, Medium, Large, X-Large)
Shown in size Petite

FINISHED MEASUREMENTS
36 (40, 44, 48, 52)" chest
22 ¼ (23 ¼, 24, 25, 25 ½)" long from shoulder along shorter side
25 ½ (26 ¼, 26 ¾, 27 ¾, 28)" long from shoulder along longer side
NOTE: Lengths are for garment measured flat; garment will stretch approximately 3" in length when worn.

YARN
Berroco Denim Silk (20% silk/80% rayon; 105 yards/50 grams): 7 (8, 9, 10, 11) skeins #1426 absinthe

NEEDLES
One pair straight needles size US 7 (4.5 mm)
Change needle size if necessary to obtain correct gauge.

NOTIONS
Row markers

GAUGE
18 sts and 26 rows = 4" (10 cm) in Stockinette st (St st)

NOTES

▎ Body of Tank is worked in one continuous piece that is knit to itself in a spiral as you work.

BODY

CO 24 sts.

Establish Border:
Row 1 (RS): K2, yo, ssk, p16, yo, ssk, k2.
Row 2: P3, yo, p2tog, k14, p1, yo, p2tog, p2.
Repeat Rows 1 and 2 twice.

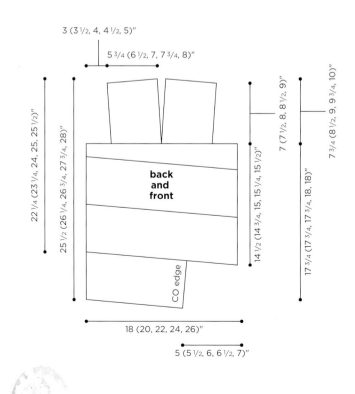

Change to Body Pattern:

Row 1 (RS): K2, yo, ssk, k16, yo, ssk, k2.

Row 2: P3, yo, p2tog, p15, yo, p2tog, p2.

Work even for 4″, ending with a WS row.

Change to Leaf Pattern:

Row 1 (RS): K1 (k1, yo, k1, yo, k1, yo, k1) in next st to increase 6 sts, k1, yo, ssk, k15, yo, ssk, k2—30 sts.

Rows 2, 4, 6 and 8: P3, yo, p2tog, p15, yo, p2tog, p8.

Rows 3, 5 and 7: K9, yo, ssk, k15, yo, ssk, k2.

Row 9: K1, ssk, k3, k2tog, k1, yo, ssk, k15, yo, ssk, k2—28 sts remain.

Row 10: P3, yo, p2tog, p15, yo, p2tog, p6.

Row 11: K1, ssk, k1, k2tog, k1, yo, ssk, k15, yo, ssk, k2—26 sts remain.

Row 12: P3, yo, p2tog, p15, yo, p2tog, p4.

Row 13: K1, sl 1, k2tog, psso, k1, yo, ssk, k15, yo, ssk, k2—24 sts remain.

Row 14: P3, yo, p2tog, p15, yo, p2tog, p2.

*Work even for 7 ¾ (8 ½, 9 ¼, 10, 10 ¾)″. Work Leaf Pattern. Repeat from * until piece measures 36 ½ (40 ½, 44 ½, 48 ¾, 52 ¾)″ from the beginning, ending with a WS row.

Join Body: Continuing to repeat from * as established, join Body to itself as follows (RS): Work as established to last st, sl 1 wyib, pick up and knit 1 st from first row of Body, psso, turn, sl 1 wyif, work to end. Next and all following RS rows: Work as established to last st, sl 1 wyib, pick up and knit 1 st 2 rows above previous picked-up st, psso, turn, sl 1 wyif, work to end.

Continue in pattern and joining as established until piece measures 90 ¼ (105 ¼, 119 ¼, 133 ¼, 147 ¼)″ from first join, ending with a WS row.

Shape Top of Body: (RS) Decrease 1 st every 14 rows 17 times as follows: Work as established to last 6 sts, k2tog, yo, ssk, k1, sl 1 wyib, pick up and knit 1 st from first row, psso, turn, sl 1 wyif, work to end—7 sts remain. BO all sts.

Lay piece flat with CO edge in front as in schematic. Place marker 5 (5 ½, 6, 6 ½, 7)″ to right of CO edge, for left side of Tank; BO edge should be in the back, 3 (3 ½, 4, 4 ½, 5)″ in from right side fold. Add or subtract rows at BO edge if necessary to get to correct length.

UPPER BODY

Mark center front and back. Mark 3 (3 ½, 4, 4 ½, 5)″ in from each side on front and back. On the back right side, the marker is at the BO edge of Body.

LEFT SHOULDER

RS facing, pick up and knit 32 (36, 38, 42, 44) sts between markers on left side of front.

Establish Pattern:

Row 1 (RS): K2, yo, ssk, k2 (2, 3, 3, 2), [p2, k2] 5 (6, 6, 7, 8) times, k1 (1, 2, 2, 1), yo, ssk, k3.

Row 2: P3, yo, p2tog, p2 (2, 3, 3, 2), [k2, p2] 5 (6, 6, 7, 8) times, p1 (1, 2, 2, 1), yo, p2tog, p2.

Work even until piece measures 7 (7 ½, 8, 8 ½, 9)″, ending with a WS row.

Shape Shoulder using short rows:

Row 1 (RS): Work 23 (23, 24, 24, 24) sts, turn.

Row 2: Yo, work to end.

Row 3: Work 19 sts, turn.

Row 4: Yo, work to end.

Row 5: Work 15 sts, turn.

Row 6: Yo, work to end.

Row 7: Work 11 sts, turn.

Row 8: Yo, work to end.

Row 9: Work 7 sts, turn.

Row 10: Yo, work to end.

Row 11: Work to end, purling each yo tog with the following st:

Work even for 7 (7 ½, 8, 8 ½, 9)″, ending with a WS row. BO all sts. Sew Shoulder between markers on left side of back. Sew end of Body to Shoulder piece.

Right Shoulder:

RS facing, pick up and knit 32 (36, 38, 42, 44) sts between markers on right side of Back. Work as for Left Shoulder. Sew Shoulder between markers on right side of Front.

Phyllotaxis Scarf

I like a scarf to be reversible as I don't like having to fuss with a "wrong side." In knitting, there are a few choices to ensure reversibility. The pattern itself might look great on both sides, like ribbing or garter stitch, or a very carefully planned cable. A tube structure is also reversible. Sure it's twice as much knitting, but knitting a scarf in a tube eliminates the common problem of curling edges as well. I had a very important third reason for making this particular scarf in a tube. The pattern is very easy to work in the round. So much so, it's practically magical. While the chart necessary to explain how to create the pattern for working back and forth would take up a full page, the circular chart is a scant 20 rounds, and while knitting, each round flows to the next without a glitch. On a mathematical note, the double spirals of twisted stitches occur in two sequential numbers from the Fibonacci sequence (see page 41), as they would in nature: There are five spirals slanting to the right and eight spirals slanting to the left so the pair from the Fibonacci sequence is 5-8.

SIZES
One size

FINISHED MEASUREMENTS
8½" wide by 60" long;
17" circumference

YARN
Harrisville Yarns Orchid Line (70% wool/25% mohair/5% silk; 245 yards/100 grams): 4 hanks #5962 ivy

NEEDLES
One 16" (40 cm) circular (circ) needle size US 8 (5 mm)
One 16" (40 cm) circular needle size US 9 (5.5 mm)
Change needle size if necessary to obtain correct gauge.

NOTIONS
Stitch markers

GAUGE
19 sts and 24 rows = 4" (10 cm) in Cable Pattern from Chart using larger needles

STITCH PATTERN
Garter Stitch in-the-Round:
(any number of sts; 2-rnd repeat)
Rnd 1: Knit.
Rnd 2: Purl.
Repeat Rnds 1 and 2 for Garter st in-the-rnd.

NOTES
▶ *Stitch Pattern:* see left.

▶ Scarf is worked as a tube in the round.

▶ When working the Chart, on even-numbered (knit) rnds, the last st worked is the first st of the next rnd. Move marker one st to the left for new beginning of rnd.

SCARF
Using smaller needles, CO 80 sts. Join for working in the rnd, being careful not to twist sts; place marker (pm) for beginning of rnd. Work in Garter st in-the-rnd for 10 rnds. Change to larger needles and knit 1 rnd. Begin Cable Pattern from Chart. Work even as established until piece measures approx 59" (or 1" short of desired length), ending with an odd-numbered row. Change to smaller needles. Work in Garter st in-the-rnd for 10 rnds. Knit 1 rnd. BO all sts purlwise.

KEY
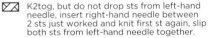

☐ Knit on RS, purl on WS.

▨ K2tog, but do not drop sts from left-hand needle, insert right-hand needle between 2 sts just worked and knit first st again, slip both sts from left-hand needle together.

▧ Knit into back of second st, then knit first and second sts together through back loops, slip both sts from left-hand needle together.

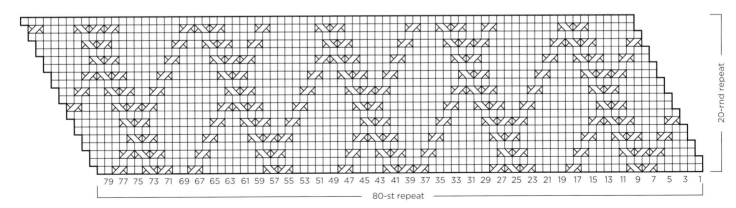

Sunflower Tam

For this tam, I wanted to make a disk with two opposing spirals, like the phyllotaxis of a sunflower, daisy, or coneflower. It may be easy for nature to follow whatever laws of physics it follows (physicists haven't figured this out) to make the opposing spirals occur with differing frequencies (usually emanating from the inside out), but for me, it was simpler to have the two spirals emanate from the same points around the edge. Still, I wanted to simulate the quirky, nonsymmetrical shapes that are formed in phyllotaxis, so I tried moving the two spirals at differing angles. This seems to simulate the right effect. The clockwise spirals move at twice the speed of the counterclockwise ones.

NOTES

▶ **Stitch Pattern:** see right.

▶ **RT:** K2tog, but do not drop sts from left-hand needle, insert right-hand needle between 2 sts just worked and knit first st again, slip both sts from left-hand needle together.

▶ **LT:** Knit into back of second st, then knit first and second sts together through back loops, slip both sts from left-hand needle together.

▶ **RT-dec:** K3tog but do not drop sts from left-hand needle, insert right-hand needle between first 2 sts just worked and knit into first st again, slip all sts from left-hand needle together.

▶ **I-cord:** *Transfer the needle with the sts to your left hand, bring the yarn around behind the work to the right-hand side; using a second dpn, knit the sts from right to left, pulling the yarn from left to right for the first st; do not turn. Slide the sts to the opposite end of the needle; repeat from * until the cord is the length desired. *Note: After a few rows, the tubular shape will become apparent.*

TAM

Using smaller circ needle, CO 100 (90) sts. Join for working in the rnd, being careful not to twist sts; place marker (pm) for beginning of rnd. Begin 1×1 Rib. Work even for 1 ½", increase 0 (10) sts on last rnd—100 (100) sts. Change to larger circ needle and work in St st for 4 rnds.

Shape Tam:

Note: Change to dpn when the work no longer fits on the circ needle.

[K16, m1] 6 times, k4—106 sts.

Knit 3 rnds even.

K8, [m1, k16] 6 times, m1, k2—113 sts.

Knit 3 rnds even.

[K16, m1] 7 times, k1—120 sts.

Knit 3 rnds even.

K4, [m1, k16] 7 times, m1, k4—128 sts.

Purl 2 rnds even.

Knit 1 rnd.

SIZES
Child (Adult)

FINISHED MEASUREMENTS
To fit Child (Adult)
18 (20)" circumference at forehead; 10 (12)" diameter

YARN
Child's Tam: Reynolds Yarns Lite Lopi (100% Icelandic wool; 109 yards/50 grams): 2 skeins #423 marine heather

Adult's Tam: Reynolds Yarns Lopi (100% Icelandic wool; 110 yards/100 grams): 2 skeins #9964 golden heather

NEEDLES
Child's Tam: One 16" (40 cm) circular (circ) needle size US 6 (4 mm)

One 16" (40 cm) circular needle size US 7 (4.5 mm)

One set of five 6" double-pointed needles (dpn) size US 7 (4.5 mm)

Adult's Tam: One 16" (40 cm) circular (circ) needle size US 8 (5 mm) (optional)

One 16" (40 cm) circular needle size US 9 (5.5 mm) (optional)

One set of five 6" double-pointed needles size US 9 (5.5 mm)

Change needle size if necessary to obtain correct gauge.

NOTIONS
Stitch marker

GAUGE
Child's Tam: 18 sts and 23 rows = 4" (10 cm) in Stockinette st (St st) using larger needles

Adult's Tam: 14 sts and 21 rows = 4" (10 cm) in Stockinette st (St st) using larger needles

STITCH PATTERN
1×1 Rib:
(multiple of 2 sts; 1-rnd repeat)
All Rnds: *K1, p1; repeat from * around.

Establish Phyllotaxis Pattern:

Rnd 1: [K7, RT, k7] 8 times.

Rnd 2: [K6, k2tog, LT, k6] 8 times—120 sts remain.

Rnd 3: [K5, RT, k1, LT, k5] 8 times.

Rnd 4: [K4, k2tog, k3, LT, k4] 8 times—112 sts remain.

Rnd 5: [K3, RT, k4, LT, k3] 8 times.

Rnd 6: [K2, k2tog, k6, LT, k2] 8 times—104 sts remain.

Rnd 7: [K1, RT, k7, LT, k1] 8 times.

Rnd 8: [K2tog, k9, LT] 8 times—96 sts remain.

Remove marker, k6, pm for new beginning of rnd.

Rnd 9: [K5, RT, k5] 8 times.

Rnd 10: [K4, k2tog, LT, k4] 8 times—88 sts remain.

Rnd 11: [K3, RT, k1, LT, k3] 8 times.

Rnd 12: [K2, k2tog, k3, LT, k2] 8 times—80 sts remain.

Rnd 13: [K1, RT, k4, LT, k1] 8 times.

Rnd 14: [K2tog, k6, LT] 8 times—72 sts remain.

Remove marker, k4, pm for new beginning of rnd.

Rnd 15: [K4, RT, k3] 8 times.

Rnd 16: [K3, k2tog, LT, k2] 8 times—64 sts remain.

Rnd 17: [K2, RT, k1, LT, k1] 8 times.

Rnd 18: [K1, k2tog, k3, LT] 8 times—56 sts remain.

Remove marker, k4, pm for new beginning of rnd.

Rnd 19: [K2, RT-dec, k2] 8 times—48 sts remain.

Rnd 20: [K1, RT, LT, k1] 8 times.

Rnd 21: [K2tog, k2, LT] 8 times—40 sts remain.

Remove marker, k2, pm for new beginning of rnd.

Rnd 22: [K2, RT, k1] 8 times.

Rnd 23: [K1, k2tog, LT] 8 times—32 sts remain.

Remove marker, k2, pm for new beginning of rnd.

Rnd 24: [K1, RT-dec] 8 times—24 sts remain.

Rnd 25: [K2tog, k1] 8 times—16 sts remain.

Remove marker, k1, pm for new beginning of rnd.

Rnd 26: [K2tog] 8 times—8 sts remain.

Remove marker, k1, pm for new beginning of rnd.

Rnd 27: [K2tog] 4 times—4 sts remain.

Knit even for 4 (5)″ or transfer all sts to one needle and work 4-st I-cord for 4 (5)″ (optional). [K2tog] twice—2 sts remain. BO all sts. Tie knot in end of tail. Weave in ends.

Chapter 5

FRACTALS*

* fractal: (n) complex geometric figure made up of patterns that repeat themselves at smaller and smaller scales, or larger and larger scales

The world around us is filled with fractals —some occur naturally and some are conjured up by mathematicians. Interestingly, some of the fractals devised by mathematicians in the past were later discovered to exist in nature. Fractal systems, both natural and mathematical, work like this: the smallest details of an object are similar in shape to its larger structures, which in turn are similar to even larger ones, and so on.

The branch of a fern plant is a good example of a natural fractal. Growing out of the stalk of the branch are leaflets that have the same shape as the branch. In turn, each leaflet is made up of smaller leaflets that have the same shape as the larger leaflet. Sometimes each of these smaller leaflets has a crenellated outline in an even smaller version of the same shape. This characteristic of similar structures at differ-ent scales is referred to as self-similarity. Rivers, corals, trees, lightening, our own blood vessels and neurons, and even the Paris Metro (although not natural) are branching fractal structures.

In mathematics, fractals are geometric representa-tions of simple equations that produce intriguing patterns. A fractal known as the Koch Snowflake is made up entirely of small triangles added to the sides of larger triangles (there is an illustration on page 143). You can also illustrate mountains and clouds using a similar additive process. Before mathematicians started to use computers in the 1960s and 1970s, fractal mathematics was merely an esoteric trick without a practical application, and it drew little interest. Now, using computers to perform the numerous repetitions of computations necessary to build a fractal, this area of mathematics has become an exciting tool with which to describe the natural world.

I am fascinated by both natural and mathematical shapes found in fractals. In this chapter, I modified a famous fractal called the Sierpinski Triangle and turned it into an openwork pattern for the Triangle Scarf (page 146). The sinuous shape of the Dragon Curve fractal adorns the yoke of the Serpentine Coat (page 136). The trim of the Coastline Camisole and Skirt (page 140) is built like the Koch Snowflake described above, with a few modifications (including a nod to the natural proportions of Garter stitch). I looked to the natural fractals of tree branches and frost when I created branching patterns for the Branching Aran Guernsey (page 122) and the Frost Jacket (page 132), respectively.

Branching Aran Guernsey

Mathematicians have found that they can approximate the branching pattern of a tree by repeating a "simple" set of rules over and over. They call this an algorithm. In word form, the basic algorithm for the columns of branching cables on this pullover is as follows: Every time a line splits into two branches, one continues on the same path as the original line and the second veers off at about a 30° angle. A mathematician would have used additional rules to specify the length of a new branch when it split off again, but I fudged a smidgen to fit the branches within the limited space of the cable columns. Still, the tree-like quality of the finished pattern is rather startling to me.

I purposefully incorporated some traditional elements of the British guernsey into this design—the drop-shoulder shaping and the simple ladder pattern between the columns of cables—and like the way they play against the naturalistic, very modern, branching cables. Beware that because of their asymmetrical nature, the branching cables do not match up at the shoulders. If that bothers you (it doesn't bother me at all), you can reverse the cable pattern for either the front or back (which is a lot more work but will give you a matching shoulder). Another solution, in keeping with guernsey tradition, would be to stop the cables, decrease the extra stitches that accommodate them, and change to Garter stitch an inch or two before the shoulder.

NOTES

❱ *Stitch Pattern:* see left.

BACK

Using smaller needles, CO 146 (158, 174, 186) sts; begin 1×1 Rib. Work even for 3″, ending with a RS row. (WS) Change to larger needles; purl 1 row, increase 0 (2, 0, 2) sts across row—146 (160, 174, 188) sts. (RS) Begin Branching Cable Pattern from Chart, as indicated for your size. Work even until piece measures 24½ (25, 25½, 26)″ from the beginning, ending with a WS row.

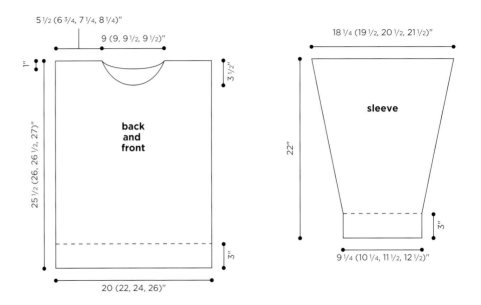

Shape Shoulders and Neck: (RS) BO 11 (12, 14, 15) sts, work 46 (52, 55, 61) sts; join a second ball of yarn and BO center 32 (32, 36, 36) sts, work to end. Working BOTH SIDES AT SAME TIME, BO 11 (12, 14, 15) sts at beginning of next row, then 10 (12, 13, 15) sts at beginning of next 6 rows and AT THE SAME TIME, BO 4 sts at each neck edge 4 times.

FRONT

Work as for Back until piece measures 22 (22½, 23, 23½)″ from the beginning, ending with a WS row.

Shape Neck: (RS) Work 63 (70, 75, 82) sts; join a second ball of yarn and BO center 20 (20, 24, 24) sts, work to end. Working BOTH SIDES AT SAME TIME, BO 5 sts at each neck edge once, 4 sts once, 3 sts twice, 2 sts twice, then decrease 1 st at each neck edge every other row 3 times, and AT THE SAME TIME, when piece measures same as for Back to shoulder, Shape shoulders as for Back.

SLEEVES (make 2)

Using smaller needles, CO 64 (72, 80, 88) sts; begin 1×1 Rib. Work even for 3″, ending with a RS row. (WS) Change to larger needles; purl 1 row. (RS) Begin Branching Cable Pattern from Chart, as indicated for your size. Work even for 1″, ending with a WS row.

Shape Sleeve: (RS) Increase 1 st each side every 4 rows 23 times, then every 6 rows 9 times, working increased sts in ribbing as indicated on chart as they become available, as follows: K1, m1, work across to last st, m1, k1—128 (136, 144, 152) sts. Work even until piece measures 22″ from the beginning. BO all sts.

FINISHING

Sew shoulder seams. Measure 9 (9¾, 10¼, 10¾)″ down from shoulder seam along each side, pm for Sleeves. Sew Sleeves between markers. Sew side and Sleeve seams.
Neckband: Using circ needle, beginning at left shoulder seam, pick up and knit 118 (118, 120, 120) sts around neckline. Join for working in the rnd, being careful not to twist sts; place marker (pm) for beginning of rnd. Begin 1×1 Rib. Work even for 3″. BO all sts in pattern. Fold neckband in half to inside and stitch to itself, being careful not to pull too tightly.

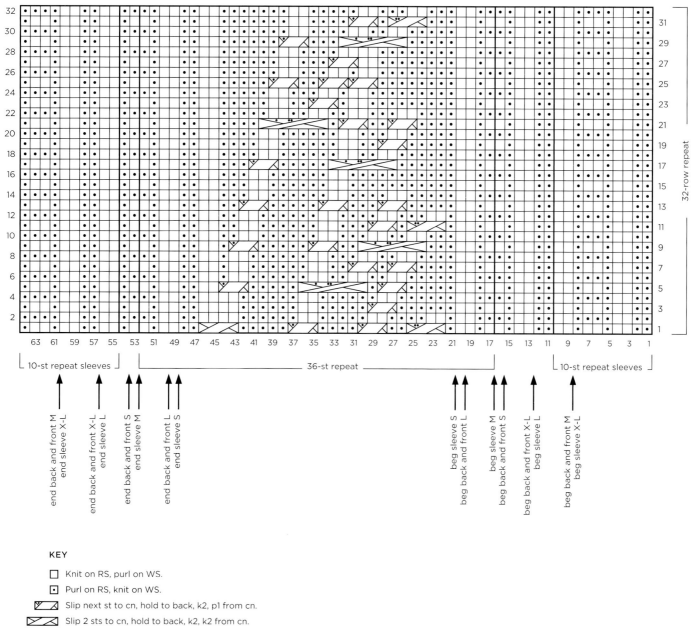

KEY

☐ Knit on RS, purl on WS.

⊡ Purl on RS, knit on WS.

Slip next st to cn, hold to back, k2, p1 from cn.

Slip 2 sts to cn, hold to back, k2, k2 from cn.

Slip 2 sts to cn, hold to back, k2, p2 from cn.

Slip 5 sts to cn, hold to back, k2, (p2, k2, p1) from cn.

Ogee Tunic

I have always admired the ogee motif, the figure made when a particular vertical wavy line and its mirror image are brought together (so they end up having an onionlike shape as shown in the illustration on page 129). Similarly loved by decorative artists through the ages, this graceful shape can be found on ancient Persian tiles, European brocades and velvets, and Indian block-print fabrics, and is echoed in the arches of Eastern architecture as well.

After studying some of the famous mathematical fractal models, like the Koch Snowflake and the Sierpinski Triangle, I constructed my own fractal pattern made of modified ogees to create this tunic. Each ogee can be divided into four smaller ogees, which can be divided into four even smaller ogees, and so on. I played a bit with the placement of the motifs and the stitchwork that fills each one (using Stockinette and Reverse Stockinette stitches, twisted stitches, and openwork) to form a pleasing pattern that fits easily on the front of this tunic. For the back, I incorporated only the half-ogees at the bottom.

SIZES
Petite (Small, Medium, Large, X-Large)
Shown in size Small

FINISHED MEASUREMENTS
32 (36, 40, 44, 48)" chest

YARN
Filatura di Crosa Zara (100% merino wool; 137 yards/50 grams): 10 (11, 13, 15, 16) balls #1719 aqua

NEEDLES
One pair straight needles size US 4 (3.5 mm)
Change needle size if necessary to obtain correct gauge.

NOTIONS
Stitch markers

GAUGE
23 sts and 32 rows = 4" (10 cm) in Stockinette st (St st)

NOTES

❱ It is essential that you get the appropriate row gauge for this pattern, so that the Front and Back will be the same length. You may want to knit the Front first in case you need to make any adjustments to the length of the Back as you work.

❱ *Decrease Row:* (RS) K3, k2tog, knit to last 5 sts, ssk, k3.

❱ The Ogee Chart for the Front splits up the center along the red line, and each side is worked separately. Join a second ball of yarn where indicated on the Chart.

❱ The 3 slip sts to either side of the neck split on the Chart form an I-cord edging.

BACK

CO 129 (143, 150, 171, 189) sts.

Establish Pattern: (RS) [K3 (5, 6, 3, 5), work Edging Chart] 6 (6, 6, 8, 8) times, k3 (5, 6, 3, 5). Next row and all WS rows: [P3 (5, 6, 3, 5), work Edging Chart] 6 (6, 6, 8, 8) times, p3 (5, 6, 3, 5). Work even until one full repeat of Chart is complete, working decreases as indicated—105 (119, 126, 139, 157) sts remain. (WS) Change to St st and decrease (decrease, work even, increase, decrease) 1 st in center—104 (118, 126, 140, 156) sts remain.

Shape Waist: (RS) Continuing in St st, work Decrease Row every 16 (16, 18, 16, 12) rows 6 (6, 5, 6, 8) times—92 (106, 116, 128, 140) sts remain. Work even until piece measures 14½" from the beginning, ending with a WS row.

Shape Armholes: (RS) BO 4 sts at beginning of next 0 (2, 2, 2, 4) rows, 3 sts at beginning of next 2 (2, 2, 4, 4) rows, then 2 sts at beginning of next 2 (2, 4, 4, 2) rows. Work Decrease Row every other row 2 (2, 2, 2, 3) times—78 (84, 90, 96, 102) sts remain. Work even until piece measures 8 (8½, 9, 9½, 10)" from beginning of armhole, ending with a WS row.

Shape Shoulders and Neck: (RS) BO 7 (8, 9, 10, 11) sts, work 22 (24, 26, 28, 30) sts; join a second ball of yarn and BO center 20 sts, work to end. Working BOTH SIDES AT SAME TIME, BO 7 (8, 9, 10, 11) sts at beginning of next row, then BO 6 (7, 8, 9, 10) sts at beginning of next 4 rows and AT THE SAME TIME, BO 5 sts at each neck edge twice.

FRONT

Work as for Back until piece measures 4½ (5, 5½, 6, 6½)" from the beginning, ending with a WS row. Mark center 78 (84, 90, 96, 102) sts. Work to marker, begin Ogee Chart as indicated for your size, work to end. Continue as established, splitting for neck where indicated on Chart, and AT THE SAME TIME, continuing waist and armhole shaping as for Back. *NOTE: If there are not enough sts to work a cable and an edge st at the armhole edge, omit the cable and work it as knit sts.* Work even until split measures 9¼", end WS row.

Shape Neck: BO 10 sts at each neck edge once, 3 sts once, 2 sts once, then decrease 1 st at each neck edge every other row 5 times—15 (18, 21, 24, 27) sts remain each side for shoulder. When piece measures same as for Back to shoulder, shape shoulders as for Back.

SLEEVES (make 2)

CO 82 (87, 92, 97, 102) sts.

Establish Pattern: (RS) [K2 (3, 4, 5, 6), work Edging Chart] 4 times, k2 (3, 4, 5, 6). Next row and all WS rows: [P2 (3, 4, 5, 6), work Edging Chart] 4 times, p3 (3, 4, 5, 6). Work even until one full repeat of Chart is complete, working decreases as indicated—66 (71, 76, 81, 86) sts remain. (WS) Change to St st and work 13 rows even, increase 1 st each side on first row—68 (73, 78, 83, 88) sts.

Shape Sleeve: (RS) Work Decrease Row this row, then every 12 rows 2 more times—62 (67, 72, 77, 92) sts remain. Work even until piece measures 11½" from the beginning, ending with a WS row. (RS) Increase one st each side this row, then every 12 rows 3 more times as follows: K3, m1, work to last 3 sts, m1, k3—70 (75, 80, 85, 90) sts. Work even until piece measures 18" from the beginning, ending with a WS row.

Shape Cap: (RS) BO 3 sts at beginning of next 2 rows, then 2 sts at beginning of next 2 rows. Work Decrease Row every other row 7 (8, 9, 10, 11) times, every 4 rows 2 times, then every other row 7 (8, 9, 10, 11) times. BO 2 sts at beginning of next 2 rows, then 3 sts at beginning of next 2 rows—18 (19, 20, 21, 22) sts remain. BO all sts.

FINISHING

Sew shoulder seams. Set in Sleeves. Sew side and Sleeve seams. **Neckband:** Beginning at left shoulder seam, pick up and knit approximately 92 sts around neckline. Knit 1 row. Purl 1 row. BO all sts knitwise.

3 1/4 (3 3/4, 4 1/4, 4 3/4, 5 1/2)"

7"

2 3/4"

8 (8 1/2, 9, 9 1/2, 10)"

9 1/4"

23 1/2 (24, 24 1/2, 25, 25 1/2)"

14 1/2"

7"

4 1/2 (5, 5 1/2, 6, 6 1/2)"

back and front

16 (18 1/2, 20 1/4, 22 1/4, 24 1/4)"

18 (20 1/2, 22, 24 1/4, 27 1/4)"

5 1/2 (6, 6 1/2, 7, 7 1/2)"

23 1/2 (24, 24 1/2, 25, 25 1/2)"

18"

sleeve

10 3/4 (11 3/4, 12 1/2, 13 1/2, 14 1/4)"

12 1/4 (13, 14, 14 3/4, 15 3/4)"

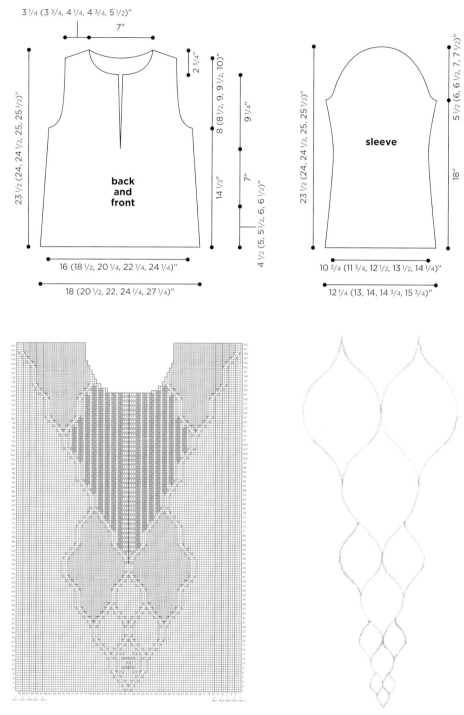

Note: Above chart illustration for reference only. See pages 130–131 for enlarged chart.

Ogee fractal before rearrangement.

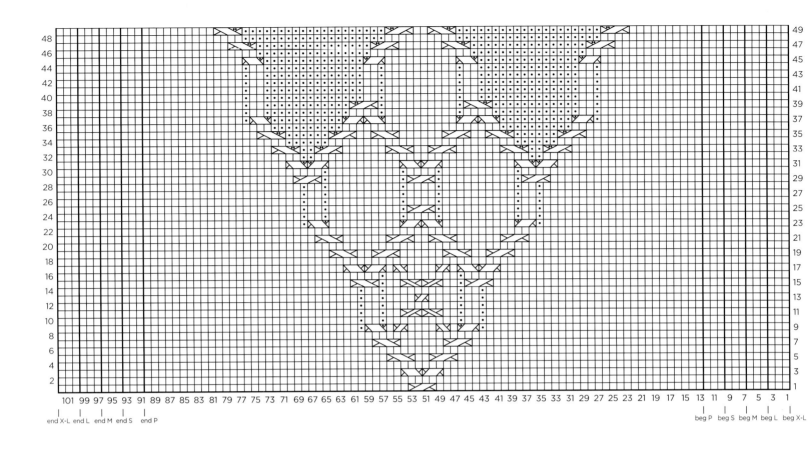

KEY

- ☐ Knit on RS, purl on WS.
- ⊡ Purl on RS, knit on WS.
- Ⅴ Slip st purlwise.
- ⊠ P2tog
- ◯ Yo
- K2tog, but do not drop sts from left-hand needle, insert right-hand needle between 2 sts just worked and knit first st again, slip both sts from left-hand needle together.
- Knit into back of second st, then knit first and second sts together through back loops, slip both sts from left-hand needle together.
- Slip next st to cn, hold to back, k2, k1 from cn.
- Slip 2 sts to cn, hold to front, k1, k2 from cn.
- Slip 2 sts to cn, hold to back, k1, k2 from cn.
- Slip next st to cn, hold to front, k2, k1 from cn.
- Slip next st to cn, hold to back, k2, p1 from cn.
- Slip 2 sts to cn, hold to front, p1, k2 from cn.
- Slip 2 sts to cn, hold to back, k2, k2tog from cn.
- Slip 2 sts to cn, hold to front, k2tog, k2 from cn.
- Slip 2 sts to cn, hold to back, k2, k2 from cn.
- Slip 2 sts to cn, hold to front, k2, k2 from cn.
- Slip 2 sts to cn, hold to back, k2, p2 from cn.
- Slip 2 sts to cn, hold to front, p2, k2 from cn.
- Slip 2 sts to cn, hold to front, k2, join second ball of yarn, k2 from cn.

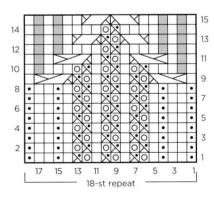

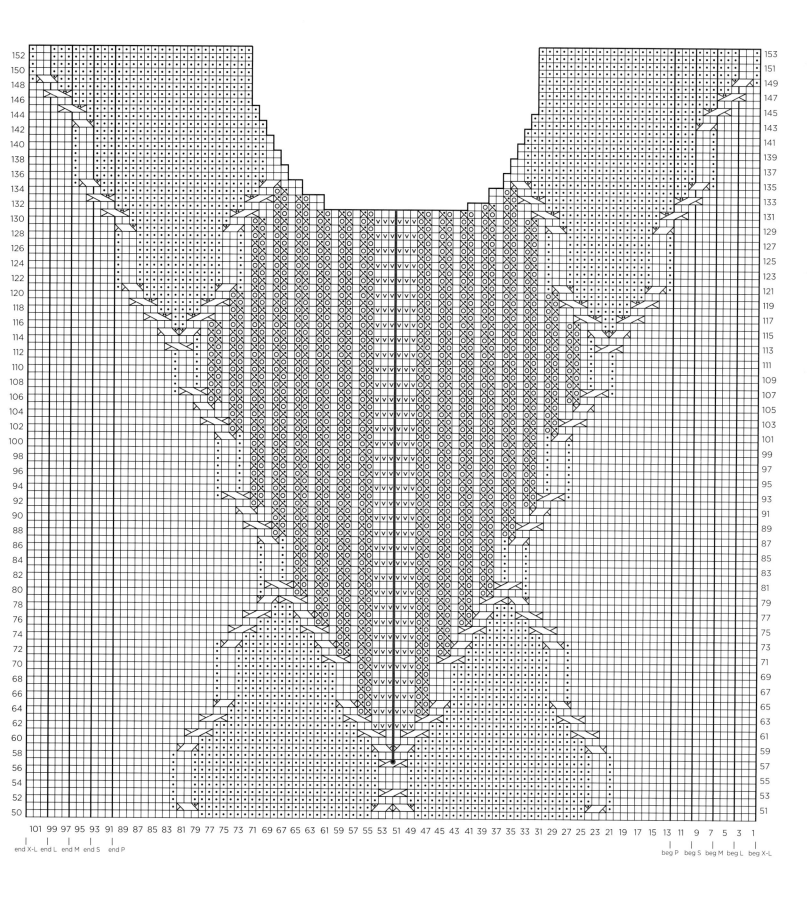

SIZES
Small (Medium, Large, X-Large)
Shown in size Small

FINISHED MEASUREMENTS
40 (44, 48, 52)" chest

YARN
Manos del Uruguay Wool (100% wool; 135 yards/100 grams): 12 (13, 15, 16) hanks #28 copper

NEEDLES
One pair straight needles size US 8 (5 mm)

One pair straight needles size US 9 (5.5 mm)

Change needle size if necessary to obtain correct gauge.

GAUGE
20 sts and 24 rows = 4" (10 cm) in Fractal Pattern from Chart using larger needles

18 sts and 20 rows = 4" (10 cm) in 1×1 Rib using larger needles

STITCH PATTERN
1×1 Rib:
(multiple of 2 sts; 1-row repeat)
All Rows: *K1, p1; repeat from * to end.

Frost Jacket

I live in a damp clapboard house along a river in New Hampshire. On frigid winter mornings moisture seeps from the wood and from the steam radiators, collecting on the cold glass windows to form spectacular frost crystals. The branching of frost crystals is fractal in nature. Larger branches collect smaller branches collect even smaller branches, and so on. So, the pattern looks similar no matter how small a section you observe. I used twisted stitches and cables to make a stylized version of the frost from my window for the body and sleeves of this jacket up to the underarm (in this case, paying little attention to the mathematical reality), then switched to a one-by-one rib for the jacket top. All of the raglan sleeve shaping is worked in the ribbing, which is a simple task (much easier than it would have been if I had maintained the twisted stitches and cables in this section).

NOTES

▶ *Stitch Pattern:* see left.

▶ This yarn is hand-dyed. To compensate for the color differences between skeins, I recommend that you work with 2 skeins at a time, alternating every other row.

BACK

Using larger needles, CO 102 (112, 124, 134) sts; purl 1 row.

Establish Pattern: (RS) K1 (selvage st, keep in St st), work Fractal Pattern from Chart to last st, k1 (selvage st, keep in St st). Work even until piece measures 17" from the beginning, ending with a RS row. (WS) Purl 1 row, decrease 9 (9, 11, 11) sts across row—93 (103, 113, 123) sts remain.

(RS) Change to 1×1 Rib. Work even for 2 rows.

Shape Armholes: (RS) BO 2 (3, 3, 4) sts at beginning of next 2 rows. Decrease 1 st each side every other row 20 (19, 18, 18) times as follows: K1, p1, ssk, work in 1×1 Rib to last 4 sts, k2tog, p1, k1. Decrease 2 sts each side every other row 4 (6, 8, 9) times as follows: K1, p1, sssk, work in 1×1 Rib to last 5 sts, k3tog, p1, k1—33 (35, 39, 43) sts remain. Work even for 2½". BO all sts in pattern.

LEFT FRONT

Using larger needles, CO 58 (58, 68, 68) sts. Work as for Back until piece measures 17" from the beginning, ending with a RS row. (WS) Purl 1 row, decrease 5 sts across row—53 (53, 63, 63) sts remain.

(RS) Change to 1×1 Rib. Work even for 2 rows.

Shape Armholes: (RS) Continuing in Rib as established BO 2 (3, 3, 4) sts, work to end. Work even for 1 row. Decrease 1 st every other row 20 (19, 18, 18) times as follows: K1, p1, ssk, work to end. Decrease 2 sts every other row 4 (6, 8, 9) times as follows: K1, p1, sssk, work to end—23 (19, 26, 23) sts remain. Work even for 2½". BO all sts in pattern.

RIGHT FRONT

Work as for Left Front to beginning of armhole shaping.

Shape Armholes: (RS) Continuing in Rib as established, work even for 1 row. BO 2 (3, 3, 4) sts, work to end. (RS) Decrease 1 st every other row 20 (19, 18, 18) times as follows: Work in 1×1 Rib to last 4 sts, k2tog, p1, k1. Decrease 2 sts every other row 4 (6, 8, 9) times as follows: Work in 1×1 Rib to last 5 sts, k3tog, p1, k1—23 (19, 25, 21) sts remain. Work even for 2½". BO all sts in pattern.

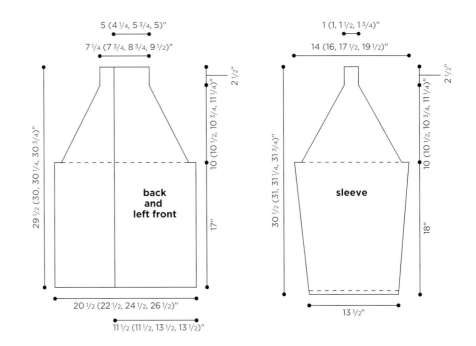

SLEEVES (make 2)

Using smaller needles, CO 60 sts; begin 1×1 Rib. Work even for ½", ending with a RS row. (WS) Purl 1 row, increase 8 sts across row—68 sts.

Establish Pattern: (RS) K1 (selvage st, keep in St st), work Fractal Pattern from Chart to last st, k1 (selvage st, keep in St st).

Shape Sleeve: (RS) Increase 1 st each side every 40 (12, 8, 6) rows 1 (6, 10, 15) times, working increased sts in pattern as they become available. Work even until piece measures 18" from the beginning, ending with a RS row. (WS) Purl 1 row, decrease 5 (7, 7, 9) sts across row—65 (73, 81, 89) sts remain.

Shape Raglan: (RS) Change to 1×1 Rib. Work even for 2 rows. Continuing in Rib as established, BO 2 (3, 3, 4) sts, work to end. Work even for 1 row. Decrease 1 st every other row 20 (19, 18, 18) times as follows: K1, p1, ssk, work to end. Decrease 2 sts every other row 4 (6, 8, 9) times as follows: K1, p1, sssk, work to end—5 (5, 7, 9) sts remain. Work even for 2½". BO all sts in pattern.

FINISHING

Sew raglan, underarm, side and Sleeve seams. **Front Bands:** Using smaller needles, pick up and knit 96 sts along front edge; begin Rev St st. Work even for 2 rows. BO all sts.

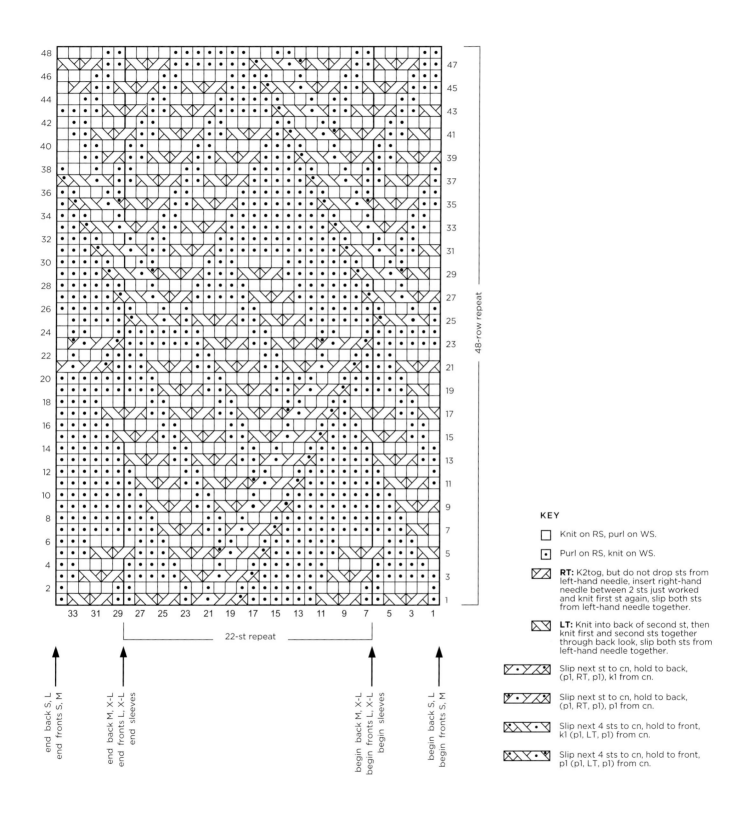

KEY

☐ Knit on RS, purl on WS.

⊡ Purl on RS, knit on WS.

RT: K2tog, but do not drop sts from left-hand needle, insert right-hand needle between 2 sts just worked and knit first st again, slip both sts from left-hand needle together.

LT: Knit into back of second st, then knit first and second sts together through back look, slip both sts from left-hand needle together.

Slip next st to cn, hold to back, (p1, RT, p1), k1 from cn.

Slip next st to cn, hold to back, (p1, RT, p1), p1 from cn.

Slip next 4 sts to cn, hold to front, k1 (p1, LT, p1) from cn.

Slip next 4 sts to cn, hold to front, p1 (p1, LT, p1) from cn.

48-row repeat

22-st repeat

end back S, L
end fronts S, M

end back M, X-L
end fronts L, X-L
end sleeves

begin back M, X-L
begin fronts L, X-L
begin sleeves

begin back S, L
begin fronts S, M

SIZES

Petite (Small, Medium, Large)
Shown in size Petite

FINISHED MEASUREMENTS

36 (40, 44, 48)" chest

YARN

Reynolds Odyssey (100% merino; 104 yards/50 grams): 16 (19, 21, 23) balls #503 brown mix (MC); 2 balls #410 sea mix (A); 2 (3, 3, 4) balls #476 granite mix (B)

NEEDLES

One pair straight needles size US 5 (3.75 mm)

One pair straight needles size US 7 (4.5 mm)

Change needle size if necessary to obtain correct gauge.

NOTIONS

Stitch holders; eight ⅞" buttons

GAUGE

20 sts and 25 rows = 4" (10 cm) in Stockinette st (St st) using larger needles

21 sts = 4" (10 cm) in 2×2 Rib using smaller needles

STITCH PATTERNS

2×2 Rib:
(multiple of 4 sts + 2; 2-row repeat)
Row 1 (RS): K2, *p2, k2; repeat from * to end.
Row 2: P2, *k2, p2; repeat from * to end.
Repeat Rows 1 and 2 for 2×2 Rib.

1×1 Rib:
(multiple of 2 sts; 1-row repeat)
All Rows: *K1, p1; repeat from * to end.

Serpentine Coat

The sinuous motif used on the yoke of this coat is a Dragon Curve, another mathematical fractal. To create a Dragon Curve, three steps are repeated over and over: to start, a unit (in this case, a stitch) is doubled and then the two units are set side by side; next, they are turned clockwise ninety degrees; the results are then doubled again and nested together diagonally. Although the figure gets bigger after each three-step transformation, the overall shape is maintained. Many seemingly complex formations in nature can actually be studied in this way.

Although the colorwork on this coat looks complex, it is very easy to achieve with variegated yarns. I used two shades for the background and one for the dragon curves. The only time two yarns are held at the same time is for the color stranding done to create the dragon curves around the yoke.

NOTES

❱ **Stitch Patterns:** see left.

❱ Body and Sleeves are worked in pieces to underarm, then joined and worked back and forth in one piece for Yoke.

BACK

Using smaller needles and MC, CO 122 (130, 142, 150) sts; begin 2×2 Rib. Work even for 3½", decrease 12 (10, 12, 10) sts across last (WS) row—110 (120, 130, 140) sts remain.

Shape Body: (RS) Change to larger needles and St st, decrease one st each side every 20 rows 10 times as follows: K3, k2tog, work to last 5 sts, ssk, k3—90 (100, 110, 120) sts remain. Work even until piece measures 36" from the beginning, ending with a WS row.

Shape Armhole: (RS) BO 7 (8, 9, 10) sts at beginning of next 2 rows—76 (84, 92, 100) sts remain. Place sts on holder for Yoke.

LEFT FRONT

Using smaller needles and MC, CO 63 (67, 75, 79) sts; begin 2×2 Rib, work to last st, k1 (selvage st, keep in St st). Work even for 3½", decrease 7 (6, 9, 8) sts across last (WS) row—56 (61, 66, 71) sts remain.

Shape Body: (RS) Change to larger needles and St st, decrease 1 st at beginning of row every 20 rows 10 times as follows: K3, k2tog, work to end—46 (51, 56, 61) sts remain. Work even until piece measures 36" from the beginning, ending with a WS row.

Shape Armhole: (RS) BO 7 (8, 9, 10) sts, work to end—39 (43, 47, 51) sts remain. Place sts on holder for Yoke.

RIGHT FRONT

Work as for Left Front, reversing patterns and shaping, and working selvage st at beginning of RS row.

SLEEVES (make 2)

Using smaller needles and MC, CO 62 (66, 70, 74) sts; begin 2×2 Rib. Work even for 3½", decrease 7 (6, 5, 4) sts across last (WS) row—55 (60, 65, 70) sts remain.

Shape Sleeve: (RS) Change to larger needles and St st, increase 1 st each side every 8 rows 8 times as follows: K2, m1, work to last 2 sts, m1, k2—71 (76, 81, 86) sts. Work even until piece measures 17" from the beginning, ending with a WS row. (RS) BO 7 (8, 9, 10) sts at beginning of next 2 rows—57 (60, 63, 66) sts. Place sts on holder for Yoke.

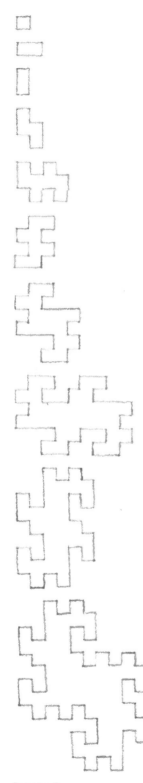

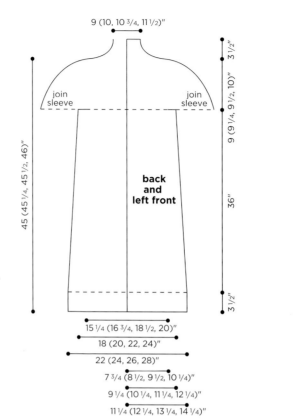

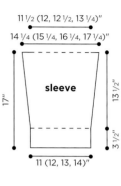

9 (10, 10 3/4, 11 1/2)"

3 1/2"

join sleeve

join sleeve

9 (9 1/4, 9 1/2, 10)"

back and left front

45 (45 1/4, 45 1/2, 46)"

36"

3 1/2"

15 1/4 (16 3/4, 18 1/2, 20)"

18 (20, 22, 24)"

22 (24, 26, 28)"

7 3/4 (8 1/2, 9 1/2, 10 1/4)"

9 1/4 (10 1/4, 11 1/4, 12 1/4)"

11 1/4 (12 1/4, 13 1/4, 14 1/4)"

11 1/2 (12, 12 1/2, 13 1/4)"

14 1/4 (15 1/4, 16 1/4, 17 1/4)"

sleeve

17"

13 1/2"

3 1/2"

11 (12, 13, 14)"

Dragon Curve

YOKE

Using yarn attached to Right Front and larger needles, knit across 39 (43, 47, 51) sts of Right Front, 57 (60, 63, 66) sts of right Sleeve, 76 (84, 92, 100) sts of Back, 57 (60, 63, 66) sts of left Sleeve and 39 (43, 47, 51) sts of Left Front—268 (290, 312, 334) sts. Purl 1 (WS) row.

Shape Yoke: (RS) Knit 1 row, decrease 4 sts across row—264 (286, 308, 330) sts remain. Work even for 1 (3, 5, 7) rows. Work Fractal Pattern from Chart, changing colors and working decreases as indicated—108 (117, 126, 135) sts remain. Change to smaller needles and B and purl 1 row, decreasing 12 (13, 14, 15, 16) sts across row—96 (104, 112, 120) sts remain.

Shape Collar: Change to 2×2 Rib as follows:

Row 1 (RS): K1, *k2, p2; repeat from * to last 3 sts, k3.

Row 2: P1, *p2, k2; repeat from * to last 3 sts, p3.

Work in Rib as established for 3 1/2". BO all sts in pattern.

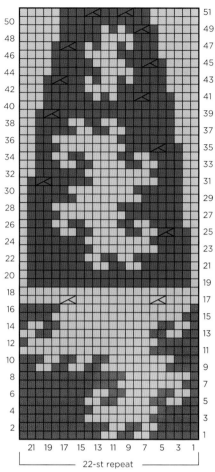

22-st repeat

KEY

NOTE: Knit on RS, purl on WS using colors.

◼ MC - brown
☐ A - sea
◼ B - granite
◺ K2tog
☐ No stitch

FINISHING

Sew underarm, side and Sleeve seams.

Button Band: Using smaller needles, CO 11 sts; begin 1×1 Rib as follows:

Row 1 (RS): K1, [k1, p1] 4 times, k2.

Row 2: K1, [p1, k1] 5 times.

Work in Rib as established until Band measures 48 (48 1/2, 49, 49 1/2)", slightly stretched. BO all sts in pattern. Place markers for buttons 1/2" from top edge, 1/2" up from beginning of collar, at Row 18 of Chart, then spaced 4 1/4" apart.

Buttonhole Band: Work as for Button Band, working buttonholes opposite button markers as follows: (RS) K2, p1, k1, yo, k2tog, [p1, k1] 2 times, k1.

Sew Button Band to Left Front edge and Buttonhole Band to Right Front edge. Sew on buttons.

Coastline Camisole and Skirt

The border on this camisole and skirt set are based upon a fractal called the Koch Snowflake, which was discovered by Helge von Koch in 1904 and then revisited in the 1970s when Benoit Mandelbrot, a mathematician famous for realizing the practical applications of fractals, discovered that it actually approximates the seemingly complex shape of a coastline. The Koch Snowflake starts with an equilateral triangle (all three sides are the same length). First, triangles with sides one third the length of the original are added to each side, then triangles with sides one third the length of the second triangles are added to each side, and so on. See the illustration on page 143.

When I saw the Koch Snowflake, I immediately came up with the idea of using it as an edging. To make this relatively easy, I knitted the bodies of the camisole and skirt, then knitted their edgings onto them. I began with the largest triangle (like Koch) by picking up stitches along the bottom edge of the garment, then decreasing one stitch at the beginning of every row (the result is not quite an equilateral triangle, but it's close enough for me). I then added two more levels of triangles. To be sure the edging would drape well and look delicate, I worked it in a single strand of yarn whereas the rest of the camisole and skirt are worked in a double strand.

NOTES

▶ *Stitch Patterns:* see right.

▶ *I-cord:* *Transfer the needle with the sts to your left hand, bring the yarn around behind the work to the right-hand side; using a second dpn, knit the sts from right to left, pulling the yarn from left to right for the first st; do not turn. Slide the sts to the opposite end of the needle; repeat from * until the cord is the length desired. *Note: After a few rows, the tubular shape will become apparent.*

CAMISOLE

BACK AND FRONT (both alike)

Using largest (size US 5) needles and 2 strands of yarn held together, CO 86 (98, 110, 122, 134) sts; begin Band Pattern. Work entire Band Pattern, decrease 3 sts across last row—83 (95, 107, 119, 131) sts remain.

Establish Pattern:

Set up Row (RS): K18 (24, 30, 32, 38), place marker (pm), [k2, yo, ssk, k1, pm, k16 (16, 16, 20, 20), pm] twice, k2, yo, ssk, knit to end.

Row 1 (WS): [Purl to marker, k1, p1, yo, p2tog, k1] 3 times, purl to end.

Row 2: [Knit to marker, k2, yo, ssk, k1] 3 times, knit to end.

Continue as established until piece measures 9½" from the beginning, ending with a WS row.

SIZES
Petite (Small, Medium, Large, X-Large)
Shown in size Small

FINISHED MEASUREMENTS
Camisole: 30 (34, 38, 42, 46)" chest
Skirt: 32 (36, 40, 44, 48)" hip; 39½ (44, 48, 52, 56½)" lower edge circumference; 30½ (31, 31½, 32, 32½)" length, including trim

YARN
Tahki Yarns Dream (80% wool/20% nylon; 262 yards/50 grams): Camisole: 5 (5, 6, 7, 8) balls; Skirt: 11 (12, 13, 14, 15) balls #03 spring green

NEEDLES
One pair straight needles in each of the following sizes: US 1 (2.5 mm), US 3 (3.25 mm), and US 5 (3.75 mm)
Two double-pointed needles (dpn) size US 3 (3.25 mm)
Change needle size if necessary to obtain correct gauge.

NOTIONS
Stitch markers

GAUGE
23 sts and 32 rows = 4" (10 cm) in Stockinette St (St st) using largest needles and 2 strands of yarn held together
36 sts and 70 rows = 4" (10 cm) in Garter St using smallest needles and single strand of yarn (trim only)

STITCH PATTERNS

Band Pattern:
(multiple of 2 sts; 37-rows)
Row 1 (WS): Knit.
Rows 2–5: Knit.
Row 6: P1, *yo, p2tog; repeat from * to last st, p1.
Rows 7–12: Knit.
Row 13: Purl.
Rows 14–24: *K1, p1; repeat from * to end.
Row 25: Purl.
Rows 26–31: Knit.
Row 32: P1, *yo, p2tog; repeat from * to last st, p1.
Rows 33–37: Knit.

2×2 Rib:
(multiple of 4 sts + 2; 2-row repeat)
Row 1 (RS): K2, *p2, k2; repeat from * to end.
Row 2: P2, *k2, p2; repeat from * to end.
Repeat Rows 1 and 2 for 2×2 Rib.

Shape Armholes: (RS) BO 5 sts at beginning of next 0 (0, 0, 2, 4) rows, 4 sts at beginning of next 2 (2, 4, 4, 4) rows, 3 sts at beginning of next 2 (4, 4, 4, 4) rows, 2 sts at beginning of next 4 (4, 4, 4, 2) rows, then decrease 1 st each side every other row 1 (2, 2, 1, 2) times—59 (63, 67, 71, 75) sts remain. Work even until piece measures 3" from beginning of armhole, ending with a RS row.

(WS) Change to size US 3 needles and purl 1 row, decrease 1 st on first row—58 (62, 66, 70, 74) sts remain. Begin 2×2 Rib. Work even for 1", ending with a WS row.

Shape Neck: (RS) Continuing in 2×2 Rib, work 17 (18, 19, 20, 21) sts; join a second ball of yarn and BO center 24 (26, 28, 30, 32) sts, work to end. Working BOTH SIDES AT SAME TIME, BO 3 sts at each neck edge twice, 2 sts twice, then decrease 1 st at each neck edge every other row twice—5 (6, 7, 8, 9) sts remain each side for shoulder. Work even until piece measures 7 (7½, 8, 8½, 9)" from beginning of armhole shaping. BO all sts.

FINISHING

Sew right shoulder seam. ***Neckband:*** Using largest (size US 5) needles and 2 strands of yarn held together, beginning at left shoulder, pick up and knit 140 (150, 158, 168, 178) sts around neck shaping. Knit 1 row. BO all sts purlwise. Sew left shoulder seam. ***Armhole Edging:*** Using largest (size US 5) needles and 2 strands of yarn held together, pick up and knit 72 (82, 92, 102, 114) sts around armhole edge. Knit 1 row. BO all sts purlwise. Sew side seams.

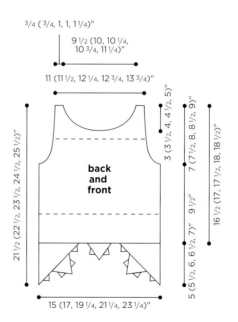

¾ (¾, 1, 1, 1¼)"

9½ (10, 10¼, 10¾, 11¼)"

11 (11½, 12¼, 12¾, 13¾)"

3 (3½, 4, 4½, 5)"

7 (7½, 8, 8½, 9)"

21½ (22½, 23½, 24½, 25½)"

back and front

16½ (17, 17½, 18, 18½)"

5 (5½, 6, 6½, 7)"   9½"

15 (17, 19¼, 21¼, 23¼)"

FRACTAL TRIM
LARGE TRIANGLES

Pm 5 (5½, 6, 6½, 7)" in from each side seam along Front and Back CO edges. Using smallest (size US 1) needles and single strand of yarn, pick up and knit 90 (99, 108, 117, 126) sts between markers. (Triangles will be centered on side seams.)

Shape Triangle: Begin Garter st, decrease 1 st every row as follows: K1, k2tog, knit to end. Work even until 2 sts remain. BO all sts.

MEDIUM TRIANGLES

Pm 3¼ (3½, 3¾, 4, 4¼)" from either side of center of the two free sides of each large Triangle. Pick up and knit 29 (31, 33, 35, 37) sts between markers. Shape as for first Triangle.

Pm 3¼ (3½, 3¾, 4, 4¼)" from either side of center of Front and Back CO edges, between large Triangles. Pick up and knit 29 (31, 33, 35, 37) sts between markers. Shape as for first Triangle.

SMALL TRIANGLES

Pm 1 (1, 1¼, 1¼, 1½)" from either side of center of the two free sides of each medium Triangle. Pick up and knit 9 (10, 11, 12, 13) sts between markers. Shape as for first Triangle.

Pm 1 (1, 1¼, 1¼, 1½)" from either side of center of the remaining open spaces along the edges of each large Triangle. Pick up and knit 9 (10, 11, 12, 13) sts between markers. Shape as for first Triangle.

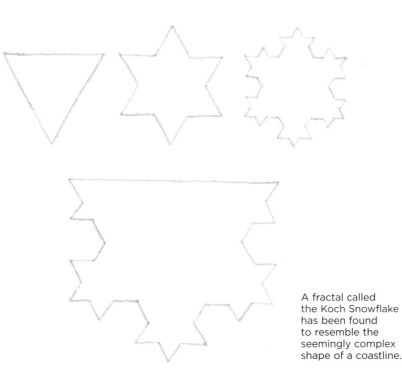

A fractal called the Koch Snowflake has been found to resemble the seemingly complex shape of a coastline.

BACK AND FRONT (both alike)

Using largest (size US 5) needles and 2 strands of yarn held together, CO 114 (126, 138, 150, 162) sts; begin Band Pattern. Work entire Band Pattern, decrease 3 sts across last row—111 (123, 135, 147, 159) sts remain.

Establish Pattern:

Set up Row (RS): K30 (32, 34, 36, 38), place marker (pm), [K2, yo, ssk, k1, pm, k18 (22, 26, 30, 34), pm] twice, k2, yo, ssk, knit to end.

Row 1 (WS): [Purl to marker, k1, p1, yo, p2tog, k1] 3 times, purl to end.

Row 2: [Knit to marker, k2, yo, ssk, k1] 3 times, knit to end.

Shape Skirt: Continuing as established, working decreases on RS rows only, decrease one st each side every 12 rows 11 times, as follows: K3, k2tog, work to last 5 sts, ssk, k3—89 (101, 113, 125, 137) sts remain. Work even until piece measures 21½" from the beginning, ending with a WS row. (RS) [Knit to marker, k2, ssk, k1] 3 times, knit to end—86 (98, 110, 122, 134) sts remain.

(WS) Change to size US 3 needles and purl 1 row. Begin 2×2 Rib. Work even for 3", ending with a WS row. (RS) Eyelet Row: K1, *ssk, yo twice, k2tog; repeat from * to last st, k1. Purl 1 row, skipping each first yo and knitting into each second yo. Purl 4 rows. BO all sts purlwise.

FINISHING

Sew side seams. Using size US 3 dpn and double strand of yarn, work 3-st I-cord for 50 (54, 58, 62, 66)". Sl 1, k2tog, psso. Break yarn, pull tight and fasten off. Weave in ends. Thread I-cord through eyelets and tie at center Front.

FRACTAL TRIM
LARGE TRIANGLES

Pm 29 (32, 34, 37, 40) sts in from each side seam (including seam st) along Front and Back CO edges. Using smallest (size US 1) needles and single strand of yarn, pick up and knit 90 (99, 108, 117, 126) sts between markers. (Triangles will be centered on side seams.) Shape as for Camisole Triangle.

Pick up and knit 90 (99, 108, 117, 126) sts between completed Triangles. Shape as for Camisole Triangle.

MEDIUM TRIANGLES

Pm 3¼ (3½, 3¾, 4, 4¼)" from either side of center of the two free sides of each large Triangle. Pick up and knit 29 (31, 33, 35, 37) sts between markers. Shape as for Camisole Triangle.

SMALL TRIANGLE

Pm 1 (1, 1¼, 1¼, 1½)" from either side of center of the two free sides of each medium Triangle. Pick up and knit 9 (10, 11, 12, 13) sts between markers. Shape as for Camisole Triangle.

Pm 1 (1, 1¼, 1¼, 1½)" from either side of center of the remaining open spaces along the edges of each large Triangle. Pick up and knit 9 (10, 11, 12, 13) sts between markers. Shape as for Camisole Triangle.

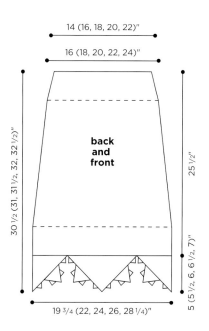

14 (16, 18, 20, 22)"

16 (18, 20, 22, 24)"

back and front

30½ (31, 31½, 32, 32½)"

25½"

5 (5½, 6, 6½, 7)"

19¾ (22, 24, 26, 28¼)"

Triangle Scarf

The triangle pattern featured in this scarf is based on a mathematical fractal called the Sierpinski Triangle. Imagine the triangle made by folding a square in half diagonally. Take a triangle out of the middle of your larger triangle, leaving equal-sized triangles in each corner. Take a triangle out of the middle of each of those triangles, etc., ad infinitum. This is very much like the familiar visual puzzle of looking at the picture of a mirror in a mirror in a mirror going on forever. An illustration of the Sierpinski Triangle appears below.

For this scarf, I placed Sierpinski Triangles (created by alternating openwork rows with knit rows) with solid Garter-stitch triangles, which makes the Sierpinski Triangles stand out. All of the openwork for the Sierpinski Triangles is done on the same side of the work, so every other row is an easy plain row. A gentle zigzag lilt occurs along the length of the finished scarf because of the difference in row gauge between the solid Garter-stitch and openwork sections.

SIZES
One size

FINISHED MEASUREMENTS
5" wide × 78" long before blocking
4" wide × 84" long after blocking

YARNS
Lang Yarns Opal (58% nylon/42% rayon; 168 yards/50 grams): 4 balls #0011 yellow

NEEDLES
One pair straight needles size US 3 (3.25 mm)

Change needle size if necessary to obtain correct gauge.

GAUGE
28 sts and 42½ rows = 4" (10 cm) in Triangle Pattern from Chart, before blocking

36 sts and 39½ rows = 4" (10 cm) in Triangle Pattern from Chart, after blocking

CO 36 sts; begin Triangle Pattern from Chart. Work even until piece measures approximately 78", ending with Row 32 or 64. BO all sts knitwise. Block piece to measurements.

Sierpinski Triangle

KEY

☐ Knit on RS, purl on WS.

· Purl on RS, knit on WS.

⊠ K2tog

⊡ Yo

64-row repeat

Chapter 6

W A V E S*

* wave: (n) a disturbance traveling through a medium without causing any permanent displacement of the medium itself

have to admit that I've used this last chapter as a bit of a catchall. I've combined projects inspired by all types of waves: water waves, chemical waves, and various fluid flow phenomena that are not technically waves but seem wave-like to me.

Water waves are familiar to all of us. Picture the swells of the ocean as a wave travels to the shore or the ripples in a pond after dropping in a pebble. In both cases, energy travels from the point of disturbance, causing a heightening and then a dip in the surface of the water. The water itself travels up and down a bit, but doesn't really travel outward with the wave. In fluids (liquids and gases), fascinating patterns occur when waves are interrupted in some way. For example, when two or more waves intersect, a new pattern, called a moiré, emerges. The arched cables of the Moiré Skirt (page 168) simulate the patterns formed by the intersecting ripples of waves in a pond.

Another type of wave is caused by chemical reactions and can be amazingly beautiful. Some chemical waves call to mind the spiraling scroll patterns one might find on a Chinese emperor's cloak. Some resemble bull's-eye targets, as on the Target Mittens (page 166). These patterns are a product of the interplay between two interdependent chemical reactions. As the material needed to fuel one reaction diminishes, the reaction itself diminishes; at the same time, a second reaction increases in frequency because the material needed for it to occur has been provided by the first reaction. In turn, the second reaction provides new material for the first reaction, and so on for quite a long time until a state of equilibrium is finally reached. The presence of the materials is seen in waxing and waning waves, spiraling

outward as the reactions continue. Similar chemical reactions may also explain natural wonders such as spiraling galaxies; differentiation of cells in embryonic development; stripes on zebras, tigers, and fish; spots on seashells, giraffes, and leopards; even the complex patterns on butterfly wings.

When fluids move around obstacles or are forced into narrow passageways, they form complicated, often beautiful, wavelike patterns. Picture the swirl that forms as you let a full basin of water go down the drain. This is called a vortex. Forced around objects or through a narrow passage-way, fluids form a series of vortexes. Another great example of vortexes is the patterns around Jupiter's great red spot. I used cables to "draw" swirling vortex shapes in the Vortex Street Pullover (page 152) and the Turbulence U-Neck Pullover (page 162).

Finally, there is a wave phenomenon called the rule of wave reflection. The rule states that when a wave of light, sound, or water hits a barrier and is reflected, the angle of reflection is the same as the angle of impact. We intuitively exploit this rule every day, when we use a car's side-view mirror or apply lipstick with a compact mirror. It's how the dentist can see our upper molars with a mirror tool and how we see our feet in the shoe store's knee-high mirror.

To visualize this rule, picture a tennis game. Hit the ball straight down into the ground and it will shoot straight back up. A long low lob will hit the ground and bounce upwards at the same low angle it hit the ground at. This rule inspired the Reflection Aran Pullover (page 156), with cables that are reflected when they "hit" an invisible central barrier.

SIZES
Petite (Small, Medium, Large, X-Large)
Shown in size Small

FINISHED MEASUREMENTS
36 (40, 44, 48, 52)" chest

YARN
Classic Elite Yarns Flash (100% mercerized cotton; 93 yards/50 grams): 14 (15, 18, 20, 22) hanks #6172 gulf green

NEEDLES
One pair straight needles size US 5 (3.75 mm)

One pair straight needles size US 7 (4.5 mm)

One 32" (80 cm) circular (circ) needle size US 7 (4.5 mm)

One 16" (40 cm) circular needle size US 5 (3.75 mm)

Change needle size if necessary to obtain correct gauge.

NOTIONS
Stitch holders

GAUGE
19 sts and 25 rows = 4" (10 cm) in Stockinette st (St st) using larger needles

STITCH PATTERNS
2×3 Rib:
(multiple of 5 sts + 2; 2-row repeat)
Row 1 (RS): *K2, p3; repeat from * to last 2 sts, k2.
Row 2: *P2, k3; repeat from * to last 2 sts, p2.

2×2 Rib:
(multiple of 4 sts + 2; 2-row repeat)
Row 1 (WS): P2, *k2, p2; repeat from * to end.
Row 2: K2, *p2, k2; repeat from * to end.
Repeat Rows 1 and 2 for 2×2 Rib.

2×2 Rib in-the-Round:
(multiple of 4 sts; 1-rnd repeat)
All Rnds: *K2, p2; repeat from * around.

A phenomenon of fluid dynamics, a vortex street is an organized pattern of spirals formed in the wake of fluid flowing past a solid object. Picture the pier of a bridge. As water flows past the obstacle, the water on the back side of the pier forms predictable patterns of wavy lines or spirals depending on the speed of the flow. (At higher speeds the patterns become chaotic.) This happens because of the disparate speeds and pressures of the passing water and of the water protected by the pier. Vortex streets are also found in clouds on earth, in the rings around Jupiter—and on the front of this pullover.

Folk wisdom says that necessity is the mother of invention, and that's surely the case with this garment. I was anxious to get a knitter started, but I didn't want to take the time to work out the center front cable pattern, meant to mimic a vortex street. So I wrote the easy rib and Stockinette stitch portions and left a wedge out of the center front, then later I knitted the center panel myself, allowing for the possibility of easy reworking if necessary. It occurs to me now that many knitters might appreciate the more complicated cable pattern being a separate piece. If a mistake is made, a bit of ripping out and reknitting goes so much faster.

NOTES

❱ *Stitch Patterns:* see left.

❱ Stockinette st portions of Body and Sleeves are worked in separate pieces to underarm, then joined and worked back and forth. Cable panel is worked separately and sewn in.

BACK

Using smaller needles, CO 112 (122, 132, 142, 152) sts; begin 2×3 Rib. Work even for 3", ending with a WS row, decrease 12 sts across last row—100 (110, 120, 130, 140) sts remain.

Shape Back: (RS) Change to larger needles and St st. Decrease 1 st each side every 10 rows 7 times as follows: K3, k2tog, work to last 5 sts, ssk, k3—86 (96, 106, 116, 126) sts remain. Work even until piece measures 16" from the beginning, ending with a RS row.

Shape Underarm: (WS) BO 7 (8, 9, 10, 11) sts at beginning of next 2 rows—72 (80, 88, 96, 104) sts remain. Break yarn and place sts on holder for Yoke.

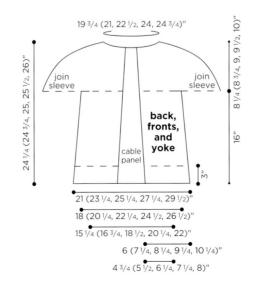

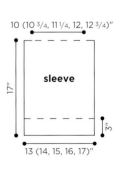

LEFT FRONT PANEL

Using smaller needles, CO 37 (42, 47, 52, 57) sts; begin 2×3 Rib. Work even for 3", ending with a WS row, decrease 8 sts across last row—29 (34, 39, 44, 49) sts remain. (RS) Change to larger needles and St st. Work even until piece measures same as for Back to underarm, ending with a WS row. (RS) BO 7 (8, 9, 10, 11) sts, work to end—22 (26, 30, 34, 38) sts remain. Break yarn and place sts on holder for Yoke.

RIGHT FRONT PANEL

Work as for Left Front Panel, reversing shaping and ending with a RS row. Place sts on holder for Yoke.

SLEEVES (make 2)

Using smaller needles, CO 72 (77, 82, 87, 92) sts; begin 2×3 Rib. Work even for 3", ending with a WS row, decrease 10 sts across last row—62 (67, 72, 77, 82) sts remain. (RS) Change to larger needles and St st. Work even until piece measures 17" from the beginning, ending with a RS row. (WS) BO 7 (8, 9, 10, 11) sts at beginning of next 2 rows—48 (51, 54, 57, 60) sts remain. Break yarn and place sts on holder for Yoke.

YOKE

Using yarn attached to Right Front Panel and larger circ needle, work across 22 (26, 30, 34, 38) sts of Right Front Panel, 48 (51, 54, 57, 60) sts of right Sleeve, 72 (80, 88, 96, 104) sts of Back, 48 (51, 54, 57, 60) sts of left Sleeve, and 22 (26, 30, 34, 38) sts of Left Front Panel—212 (234, 256, 278, 300) sts. Begin St st; purl 1 row. (RS) Knit 1 row, decrease 2 (0, 4, 2, 2) sts across row—210 (234, 252, 276, 298) sts remain. Work even for 4 (4½, 5, 5, 5½)", ending with a WS row.

Shape Yoke:

(RS) *[K4, k2tog]; repeat from * to end of row—175 (195, 210, 230, 240) sts remain. Work even for 2 (2, 2, 2½, 2½)", ending with a WS row.

(RS) *[K3, k2tog]; repeat from * to end of row—140 (156, 168, 184, 192) sts remain. Work even for 7 rows.

(RS) *[K2, k2tog]; repeat from * to end of row—105 (117, 126, 138, 144) sts remain. Work even for 3 rows.

(RS) *[K2, k2tog]; repeat from * to last 1 (1, 2, 2, 0) sts, k1 (1, 2, 2, 0)—79 (88, 95, 104, 108) sts remain. Place sts on holder for Neck.

VORTEX CABLE PANEL

Note: Panel is worked from the top down.

CO 26 sts.

Establish Pattern: (RS) K2 [p2, k2] twice, work across 6 sts of Vortex Cable Chart, [k2, p2] twice, k2. (WS) P2, [k2, p2] twice, work across 6 sts of Chart, [p2, k2] twice, p2. Work even as established until you have completed Row 167 of Chart, working increases as indicated in Chart—54 sts. (WS) Change to smaller needles and 2×2 Rib [begin p2], working last 2 rows of Chart as indicated. BO all sts in pattern.

FINISHING

Block pieces to measurements. Sew Cable Panel to front opening. **Neckband:** Using smaller circ needle, pick up and knit 24 sts across Cable Panel, work across 79 (88, 95, 104, 108) sts from Yoke holder—103 (112, 119, 128, 132) sts. Join for working in the rnd, being careful not to twist sts; pm for beginning of rnd. Begin 2×2 Rib in-the-rnd, decrease 1 (0, 1, 0, 0) sts on first rnd—104 (112, 120, 128, 132) sts remain. Work even for 8". BO all sts in pattern. Sew underarm, side and Sleeve seams.

KEY

☐ Knit on RS, purl on WS.

• Purl on RS, knit on WS.

☒ Make 1 knitwise.

● Make Bobble: [K1-f/b, k1f/b] in same st to increase to 4 sts, slip sts back onto left-hand needle, p4, slip sts back onto left-hand needle, k4, pull second, third, fourth, then fifth sts one at a time over first st and off needle.

▱ K2tog, but do not drop sts from left-hand needle, insert right-hand needle between 2 sts just worked and knit first st again, slip both sts from left-hand needle together.

▱ Knit into back of second st, then knit first and second sts together through back loops, slip both sts from left-hand needle together.

▱ Slip next st to cn, hold to back, k2, k1 from cn.

▱ Slip 2 sts to cn, hold to front, k1, k2 from cn.

▱ Slip next st to cn, hold to back, k2, p1 from cn.

▱ Slip 2 sts to cn, hold to front, p1, k2 from cn.

▱ Slip 2 sts to cn, hold to back, k2, k2 from cn.

▱ Slip 2 sts to cn, hold to front, k2, k2 from cn.

▱ Slip 2 sts to cn, hold to back, k2, p2 from cn.

▱ Slip 2 sts to cn, hold to front, p2, k2 from cn.

Reflection Aran Pullover

Inspired by the rule of wave reflection, the cables in this pullover "reflect" off of the edges of the center panel. A subtle pattern is formed by the use of two different stitches. Above the ribbing, all knit-four sections move from right to left, and all four-stitch mini cables move in the opposite direction, from left to right. As the cables reach the edge of the center panel, they are turned back into the center at the same angle as the approach. Soon we see that the knit-four sections are all on one side of the panel and the mini cables are all on the other. After they "hit the wall" again they mix again before separating out on opposite sides. Finally, they make their way back to their original positions and start over.

NOTES

❱ *Stitch Patterns:* see right.

❱ *RT:* K2tog, but do not drop sts from left-hand needle, insert right-hand needle between 2 sts just worked and knit first st again, slip both sts from left-hand needle together.

BACK

Using smaller needles, CO 110 (118, 126) sts; begin 1×1 Rib. Work even for 3", ending with a WS row; place marker (pm) 8 (12, 16) sts in from each edge. (RS) Knit 1 row, increase 28 sts between markers—138 (146, 154) sts.

Establish Pattern:

Row 1 (WS): Work 8 (12, 16) sts in Moss st, work Section C from Chart A over 21 sts, [k1, p2, k1] 20 times, work Section A from Chart A over 21 sts, work 8 (12, 16) sts in Moss st [begin with p1].

Row 2: Work 8 (12, 16) sts in Moss st, work Section A from Chart A over 21 sts, [P1, RT, p1] 20 times, work Section C from Chart A over 21 sts, work 8 (12, 16) sts in Moss st. Work even as established until piece measures 26 ½ (27, 27 ½)" from the beginning. BO all sts.

FRONT

Using smaller needles, CO 110 (118, 126) sts; begin 1×1 Rib. Work even for 3", ending with a WS row. (RS) K8 (12, 16), [k1, k1-f/b] 47 times, k8 (12, 16)—157 (165, 173) sts.

Establish Pattern: (WS) Work 8 (12, 16) sts in Moss st, work Section C from Chart A over 21 sts, work entire Chart B over 99 sts, work Section A from Chart A over 21 sts, work 8 (12, 16) sts in Moss st [begin with p1]. Work even as established until piece measures 23 ½ (24, 24 ½)" from the beginning, ending with a WS row.

Shape Neck: (RS) Work 63 (67, 71) sts; join a second ball of yarn and BO center 31 sts, work to end. Working BOTH SIDES AT SAME TIME, BO 5 sts at each neck edge 4 times—43 (47, 51) sts remain each side for shoulders. Work even until piece measures 26 ½ (27, 27 ½)" from the beginning. BO all sts.

SIZES
Medium (Large, X-Large)
Shown in size X-Large

FINISHED MEASUREMENTS
45 (48, 52)" chest

YARN
Harrisville Highland Style (100% wool; 200 yards/100 grams): 9 (10, 11) skeins #8469 cypress

NEEDLES
One pair straight needles size US 6 (4 mm)
One pair straight needles size US 8 (5 mm)
One 16" (40 cm) circular (circ) needle size US 6 (4 mm)
Change needle size if necessary to obtain gauge.

NOTIONS
Stitch and row markers

GAUGE
18 sts and 28 rows = 4" (10 cm) in Moss st using larger needles
32 sts = 4" (10 cm) in Cable Pattern from Chart A using larger needles

STITCH PATTERNS
1×1 Rib:
(multiple of 2 sts; 1-row repeat)
All Rows: *K1, p1; repeat from * to end.

Moss Stitch:
(multiple of 2 sts; 4-row repeat)
Row 1 (WS): *K1, p1; repeat from * to end.
Row 2: Purl the purls and knit the knits as they face you.
Row 3: Purl the knits and knit the purls as they face you.
Row 4: Repeat Row 2.
Repeat Rows 1–4 for Moss st.

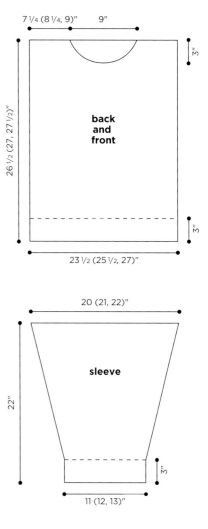

7 1/4 (8 1/4, 9)"   9"

3"

back
and
front

26 1/2 (27, 27 1/2)"

3"

23 1/2 (25 1/2, 27)"

20 (21, 22)"

22"

sleeve

3"

11 (12, 13)"

SLEEVES (make 2)

Using smaller needles, CO 56 (60, 64) sts; begin 1×1 Rib. Work even for 3", ending with a WS row. (RS) Change to larger needles and knit 1 row, increase 8 sts across first row—64 (68, 72) sts. (WS) Work 9 (11, 13) sts in Moss st, begin Cable Pattern from Chart A, work Sections A, B and C, work 9 (11, 13) sts in Moss st [begin with p1]. Work even for 1", ending with a WS row.

Shape Sleeve: (RS) Increase 1 st each side every 4 rows 3 times, then every 6 rows 18 times, working increased sts in Moss st as they become available, as follows: Work 1, m1, work to last st, m1, work 1—106 (110, 114) sts. Work even until piece measures 22" from the beginning. BO all sts.

FINISHING

Sew shoulder seams. Measure down 10 (10½, 11)" from shoulder seam along each side and place markers. Sew Sleeves between markers. Sew side and Sleeve seams.

Neckband: Using circ needle, beginning at left shoulder seam, pick up and knit 104 sts around neck shaping. Join for working in the rnd, being careful not to twist sts; pm for beginning of rnd. Begin 1×1 Rib. Work even for 1¼". BO all sts in pattern.

CHART A
DIAMOND CHART

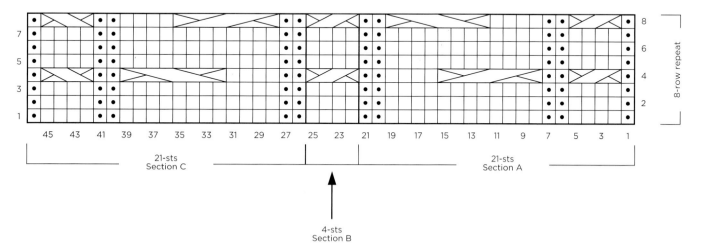

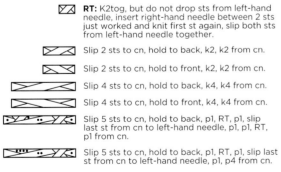

Chart B grid with row numbers: right side (even) 56, 54, 52, 50, 48, 46, 44, 42, 40, 38, 36, 34, 32, 30, 28, 26, 24, 22, 20, 18, 16, 14, 12, 10, 8, 6, 4, 2. Left side (odd) 55, 53, 51, 49, 47, 45, 43, 41, 39, 37, 35, 33, 31, 29, 27, 25, 23, 21, 19, 17, 15, 13, 11, 9, 7, 5, 3, 1.

Bottom stitch numbers: 99 97 95 93 91 89 87 85 83 81 79 77 75 73 71 69 67 65 63 61 59 57 55 53 51 49 47 45 43 41 39 37 35 33 31 29 27 25 23 21 19 17 15 13 11 9 7 5 3 1

KEY

□ Knit on RS, purl on WS.

· Purl on RS, knit on WS.

RT: K2tog, but do not drop sts from left-hand needle, insert right-hand needle between 2 sts just worked and knit first st again, slip both sts from left-hand needle together.

Slip 2 sts to cn, hold to back, k2, k2 from cn.

Slip 2 sts to cn, hold to front, k2, k2 from cn.

Slip 4 sts to cn, hold to back, k4, k4 from cn.

Slip 4 sts to cn, hold to front, k4, k4 from cn.

Slip 5 sts to cn, hold to back, p1, RT, p1, slip last st from cn to left-hand needle, p1, p1, RT, p1 from cn.

Slip 5 sts to cn, hold to back, p1, RT, p1, slip last st from cn to left-hand needle, p1, p4 from cn.

Slip 5 sts to cn, hold to back, p1, RT, p1, slip last st from cn to left-hand needle, p1, k4 from cn.

Slip 5 sts to cn, hold to back, k4, slip last st from cn to left-hand needle, p1, p1, RT, p1 from cn.

Slip 5 sts to cn, hold to back, k4, slip last st from cn to left-hand needle, p1, p4 from cn.

Slip 5 sts to cn, hold to back, k4, slip last st from cn to left-hand needle, p1, k4 from cn.

Slip 5 sts to cn, hold to front, p1, RT, p1, slip last st from cn to left-hand needle, p1, p1, RT, p1 from cn.

Slip 5 sts to cn, hold to front, p4, slip last st from cn to left-hand needle, p1, p1, RT, p1 from cn.

Slip 5 sts to cn, hold to front, k4, slip last st from cn to left-hand needle, p1, p1, RT, p1 from cn.

Slip 5 sts to cn, hold to front, p1, RT, p1, slip last st from cn to left-hand needle, p1, p4 from cn.

Slip 5 sts to cn, hold to front, p4, slip last st from cn to left-hand needle, p1, k4 from cn.

Slip 5 sts to cn, hold to front, k4, slip last st from cn to left-hand needle, p1, k4 from cn.

CHART B (continued)

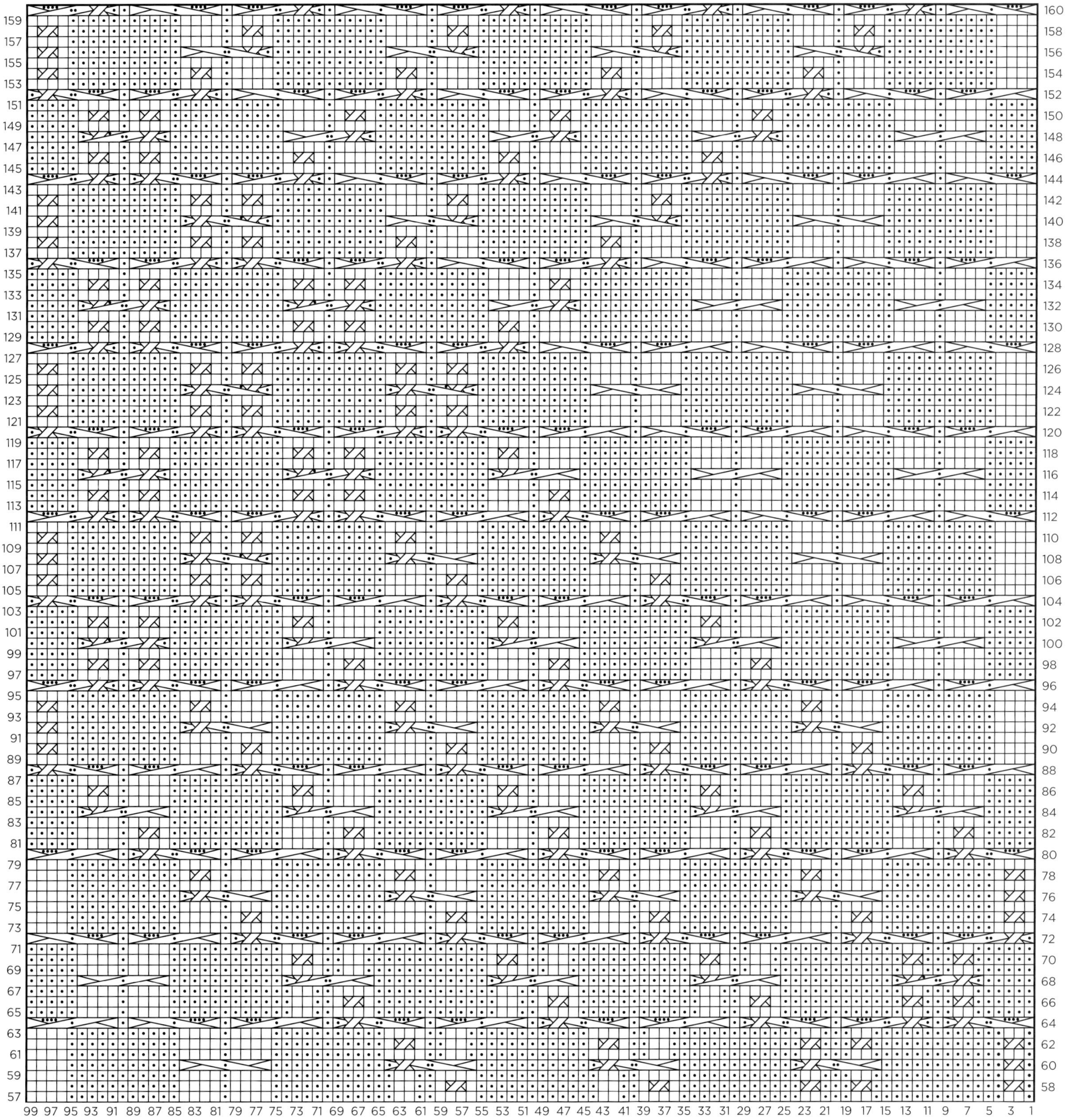

Turbulence U-Neck Pullover

Turbulent swirling liquids form interesting patterns. The cable on the center front of this pullover is loosely based on a photo I found of fluid rushing into a funnel, entering from the narrow end. The gently curved low-lying neckline and the cable pattern highlight (without accentuating) good cleavage. The lightweight worsted yarn worked at the relatively small gauge of 5 ½ stitches to the inch contributes to its flattering fit.

SIZES
Petite (Small, Medium, Large)
Shown in size Petite

FINISHED MEASUREMENTS
36 (40, 44, 48)" chest

YARN
Berroco Softwist (59% rayon/41% wool; 100 yards/50 grams): 9 (11, 12, 14) hanks #9465 twine

NEEDLES
One pair straight needles size US 4 (3.5 mm)

One pair straight needles size US 6 (4 mm)

Change needle size if necessary to obtain gauge.

NOTIONS
Stitch markers

GAUGE
22 sts and 30 rows = 4" (10 cm) in Stockinette st (St st) using larger needles

STITCH PATTERN
Half Twisted Rib:
(even number of sts; 1-row repeat)
All Rows: *K1-tbl, p1, repeat from * to end.

NOTES

❱ *Stitch Pattern:* see left.

BACK

Using smaller needles, CO 100 (112, 124, 136) sts; begin Half Twisted Rib. Work even for 1½", ending with a WS row. (RS) Change to larger needles and St st. Work even until piece measures 12" from the beginning, ending with a WS row.

Shape Armholes: (RS) BO 4 sts at beginning of next 2 (2, 4, 4) rows, 3 sts at beginning of next 2 (4, 4, 6) rows, 2 sts at beginning of next 4 rows, then decrease one st each side every other row 3 (3, 2, 2) times as follows: K2, k2tog, work to last 4 sts, ssk, k2—72 (78, 84, 90) sts remain. Work even until piece measures 7 ¼ (7 ¾, 8 ¼, 8 ¾)" from beginning of armhole shaping, ending with a WS row.

Shape Neck: (RS) Work 16 (18, 20, 22) sts; join a second ball of yarn and BO center 40 (42, 44, 46) sts, work to end. Working BOTH SIDES AT SAME TIME, BO 6 sts at each neck edge twice—4 (6, 8, 10) sts remain each side for shoulders. BO all sts.

FRONT

Using smaller needles, CO 100 (112, 124, 136) sts; begin Half Twisted Rib. Work even for 1½", ending with a RS row.

Establish Pattern:

Set-up Row: (WS) P46 (52, 58, 64), k2, p4, k2, p46 (52, 58, 64).

Row 1: Work in St st over 46 (52, 58, 64) sts, work Center Cable Chart over 8 sts, work in St st to end.

Work even until piece measures 10 (10 ½, 11, 11 ½)" from the beginning, ending with Row 4 of Chart.

Establish Pattern:

Work 24 (30, 36, 42) sts, place marker (pm), work Turbulence Cable Chart over center 52 sts, pm, work to end. Work even as established until Chart is complete, and AT THE SAME TIME, when piece measures same as for Back to armhole shaping, Shape Armhole as for Back—72 (78, 84, 90) sts remain. Knit 1 row, decrease 4 sts between markers—68 (74, 80, 86) sts remain. Purl 1 row.

Shape Neck: (RS) Work to 1 st before marker, k2tog [move marker to left of k2tog], k3; join a second ball of yarn and BO center 40 sts, k3, ssk [move marker to right of ssk], work to end. Working BOTH SIDES AT SAME TIME, work 1 row even. Decrease 1 st at each neck edge every other row 0 (1, 3, 5) times, then every 4 rows 9 (9, 8, 7) times as follows: On right side, work to 2 sts before marker, k2tog, work to end of right side; on left side, k3, ssk, work to end—4 (6, 8, 10) sts remain each side for shoulders. Work even until piece measures same as for Back to shoulder. BO all sts.

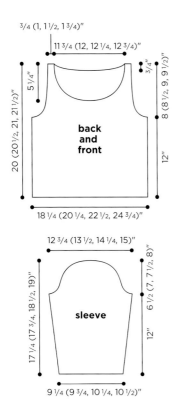

3/4 (1, 1 1/2, 1 3/4)"

11 3/4 (12, 12 1/4, 12 3/4)"

3/4"

5 1/4"

back and front

20 (20 1/2, 21, 21 1/2)"

8 (8 1/2, 9, 9 1/2)"

12"

18 1/4 (20 1/4, 22 1/2, 24 3/4)"

12 3/4 (13 1/2, 14 1/4, 15)"

sleeve

17 1/4 (17 3/4, 18 1/2, 19)"

6 1/2 (7, 7 1/2, 8)"

12"

9 1/4 (9 3/4, 10 1/4, 10 1/2)"

KEY

☐ Knit on RS, purl on WS.

⊡ Purl on RS, knit on WS.

Slip next st to cn, hold to back, k2, p1 from cn.

Slip 2 sts to cn, hold to front, p1, k2 from cn.

Slip 2 sts to cn, hold to back, k2, k2 from cn.

Slip 2 sts to cn, hold to front, k2, k2 from cn.

Slip 1 st to cn, hold to back, k3, k1 from cn.

Slip 3 sts to cn, hold to front, k1, k3 from cn.

Slip 1 sts to cn, hold to back, k3, p1 from cn.

Slip 3 sts to cn, hold to front, p1, k3 from cn.

Slip 2 sts to cn, hold to back, k2, p2 from cn.

Slip 2 sts to cn, hold to front, p2, k2 from cn.

Slip 2 sts to cn, hold to back, k3, k2 from cn.

Slip 3 sts to cn, hold to front, k2, k3 from cn.

Slip 2 sts to cn, hold to back, k3, p2 from cn.

Slip 3 sts to cn, hold to front, p2, k3 from cn.

Slip 3 sts to cn, hold to back, k3, k3 from cn.

Slip 3 sts to cn, hold to front, k3, k3 from cn.

Slip 3 sts to cn, hold to back, k3, p3 from cn.

Slip 3 sts to cn, hold to front, p3, k3 from cn.

SLEEVES (make 2)

Using smaller needles, CO 52 (54, 56, 58) sts; begin Half Twisted Rib. Work even for 1½", ending with a WS row.

Shape Sleeve: (RS) Change to larger needles and St st. Increase 1 st each side every 6 rows 9 (10, 11, 12) times as follows: K2, m1, work to last 2 sts, m1, k2—70 (74, 78, 82) sts. Work even until piece measures 12″ from the beginning, ending with a WS row.

Shape Cap: (RS) BO 3 sts at beginning of next 2 rows, 2 sts at beginning of next 2 rows, then decrease 1 st each side every other row 5 times, every 4 rows 5 (6, 7, 8) times, then every other row 5 times, as follows: K2, k2tog, work to last 4 sts, ssk, k2. (RS) BO 2 sts at beginning of next 2 rows, then 3 sts at beginning of next 2 rows—20 (22, 24, 26) sts remain. BO all sts.

FINISHING

Sew right shoulder. Using smaller needles, beginning at left shoulder, pick up and knit 170 (174, 178, 182) sts around neck shaping. (WS) Knit 1 row. BO all sts purlwise. Sew left shoulder seam. Set in Sleeves. Sew side and Sleeve seams.

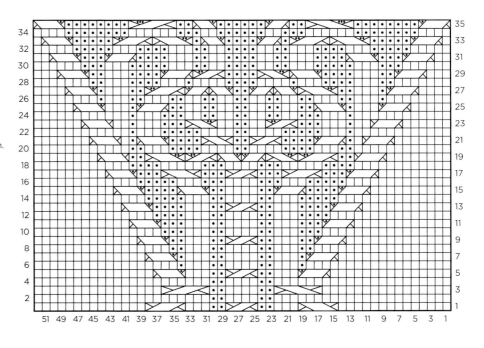

CENTER CABLE CHART

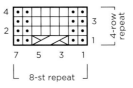

4-row repeat

8-st repeat

Target Wave Mittens

The targets on these mittens were inspired by the look of traveling chemical waves. Each mitten is worked flat with stripes in the rib and fingertips. When working the hand, a semi-circle is left out where the thumb pad and thumb ought to be. Later, stitches are picked up to create these missing parts and work the striking target motif simultaneously.

SIZES
Child's Small (Medium, Large)
Shown in size Medium

FINISHED MEASUREMENTS
6 (6 ¾,7 ½)" circumference × 8 ¼
(8 ½, 9 ¼)" long

YARN
Goddess Yarns Phoebe (100% baby alpaca; 73 yards/50 grams): 1 skein #C740 lagoon heather (MC); 1 skein #8325 fern (CC)

NEEDLES
One pair straight needles size US 6 (4 mm)
One pair straight needles size US 8 (5 mm)
Change needle size if necessary to obtain correct gauge.

GAUGE
20 sts and 25 rows = 4" (10 cm) in Stockinette st (St st) using larger needles

STITCH PATTERN
2×2 Rib:
(multiple of 4 sts + 2; 2-row repeat)
Row 1 (RS): K2, *p2, k2; repeat from * to end.
Row 2: P2, *k2, p2; repeat from * to end.

MITTEN (make 2)

Using smaller needles and CC, CO 30 (34, 38) sts; begin 2×2 Rib (see left). Work even for 2 rows. (RS) Continuing in 2×2 Rib, *change to MC and work even for 2 rows. Change to CC and work even for 2 rows. Repeat from * 2 times. Change to MC and work even for 1 row. (WS) Change to larger needles and work in St st for 1 (1, 3) rows.

Shape Opening for Thumb Target: (RS) Change to St st, BO 3 sts at beginning of next 2 rows—24 (28, 32) sts remain. Shape Opening as follows:

Row 1 (RS): K1, k2tog, work to last 3 sts, ssk, k1 (22, 26, 30) sts remain.

Rows 2 and all WS Rows: Purl.

Rows 3-8: Repeat Rows 1 and 2 3 times—16 (20, 24) sts remain after Row 7.

Row 9, 11 and 13: Knit.

Row 15: K1, m1, work to last st, m1, k1—18 (22, 26) sts.

Row 16: Purl.

Rows 17-22: Repeat Rows 15 and 16 3 times—24 (28, 32) sts after Row 21.

(RS) CO 3 sts at end of next 2 rows—30 (34, 38) sts. Work even for 0 (2, 4) rows. Change to CC and work even for 2 rows.

Shape Fingertip Target: (WS) Continuing in St st, change to MC; *k3, k2tog; repeat from * to last 0 (4, 3) sts, k0 (4, 3)—24 (28, 31) sts remain. Purl 1 row. Change to CC and work even for 2 rows.

Change to MC; *k2, k2tog; repeat from * to last 0 (0, 3) sts, k0 (0, 3)—18 (21, 24) sts remain. Purl 1 row.

Change to CC; * k2tog; repeat from * to last 0 (1, 0) st, k0 (1, 0)—9 (11, 12) sts remain. Purl 1 row.

Change to MC; *k2tog; repeat from * to last 1 (1, 0) st, k1 (1, 0)—4 (5, 6) sts remain. Purl 1 row. Break yarn, thread through remaining sts, pull tight and fasten off. Sew seam to top of opening for Thumb Target.

THUMB TARGET

Using larger needles and CC, pick up and knit 58 sts around opening for Thumb Target. Purl 1 row.

Change to MC; *k4, k2tog; repeat from * to last 4 sts, k4—49 sts remain. Purl 1 row.

Change to CC; work even for 2 rows.

Change to MC; *k3, k2tog; repeat from * to last 4 sts, k4—40 sts remain. Purl 1 row.

Change to CC; *k2, k2tog; repeat from * to last 4 sts, k4—31 sts remain. Purl 1 row.

Change to MC; *k1, k2tog; repeat from * to last 4 sts, k4—22 sts remain. Purl 1 row.

Change to CC; *k1, k2tog; repeat from * to last 4 sts, k4—16 sts remain. Purl 1 row.

Change to MC; decrease 4 (2, 0) sts across row—12 (14, 16) sts remain. Purl 1 row.

*Change to CC; work even for 2 rows. Change to MC; work even for 2 rows. Repeat from * 2 (3, 4) times. Change to CC; knit 1 row. (WS) *P2tog; repeat from * to end—6 (7, 8) sts remain. Break yarn, thread through remaining sts, pull tight, fasten off. Sew Thumb and side seam.

Moiré Skirt

In nature a moiré pattern is formed when two different waves run into each other. The simplest kind of moiré can be seen when two pebbles are dropped into a still pond, and the resulting ripples run into each other and overlap. I based this six-gore skirt on the pond-ripple idea. Six identical panels each have cabled arcs intersecting to form a center lozenge. If you don't want to work the cables, make the easy variation, which is all Stockinette stitch except for the ribbed waistband.

NOTES

▌ *Stitch Pattern:* see right.

▌ Easy Skirt is worked entirely in St st to the Waistband. Follow Moiré Pattern Chart for decreases only; do not work Moiré Pattern.

▌ Easy Skirt seams will all be on the RS of the Skirt, and will then be finished with single crochet.

MOIRÉ SKIRT

GORES (make 6)

CO 38 (42, 46, 50, 54) sts; begin Moiré Pattern from Chart, beginning and ending as indicated for your size, and working decreases as shown—24 (28, 32, 36, 40) sts remain. BO all sts knitwise.

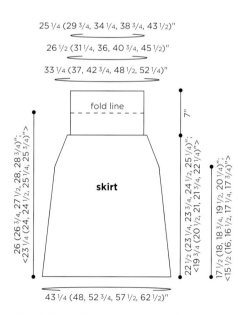

25 1/4 (29 3/4, 34 1/4, 38 3/4, 43 1/2)"

26 1/2 (31 1/4, 36, 40 3/4, 45 1/2)"

33 1/4 (37, 42 3/4, 48 1/2, 52 1/4)"

fold line

7"

skirt

26 (26 3/4, 27 1/2, 28, 28 3/4)"
<23 1/4 (24, 24 1/2, 25 1/4, 25 3/4)">

22 1/2 (23 1/4, 23 3/4, 24 1/2, 25 1/4)"
<19 3/4 (20 1/2, 21, 21 3/4, 22 1/4)">

17 1/2 (18, 18 3/4, 19 1/2, 20 1/4)"
<15 1/2 (16, 16 1/2, 17 1/4, 17 3/4)">

43 1/4 (48, 52 3/4, 57 1/2, 62 1/2)"

NOTE: Easy Skirt measurements are shown between <>. Where there is only one set of measurements, it applies to both Skirts.

SIZES

Petite (Small, Medium, Large, X-Large)
Shown in size Petite

FINISHED MEASUREMENTS

Moiré Skirt: 33 1/4 (37, 42 3/4, 48 1/2, 52 1/4)" hip
26 (26 3/4, 27 1/2, 28, 28 3/4)" long
Easy Skirt: 33 1/4 (37, 42 3/4, 48 1/2, 52 1/4)" hip
23 1/4 (24, 24 1/2, 25 1/4, 25 3/4)" long

YARN

Berroco Zen (40% cotton/60% nylon; 110 yards/50 grams)
Moiré Skirt: 7 (9, 10, 11, 13) balls #8242 Kawakubo blue
Easy Skirt: 7 (9, 10, 11, 13) balls #8139 Osaka mix

NEEDLES

One pair straight needles size US 6 (4 mm)

One pair straight needles size US 8 (5 mm)

One 24" (60 cm) circular (circ) needle size US 6 (4 mm)

NOTIONS

Stitch marker
Easy Skirt: Crochet hook size US J/10 (6 mm)

GAUGE

Moiré Skirt: 20 sts and 23 rows = 4" (10 cm) in Moiré Pattern from Chart using larger needles

Easy Skirt: 20 sts and 26 rows = 4" (10 cm) in Stockinette st (St st) using larger needles

STITCH PATTERN

2×2 Rib:
(multiple of 4 sts; 1-rnd repeat)
All Rnds: *K2, p2; repeat from * around.

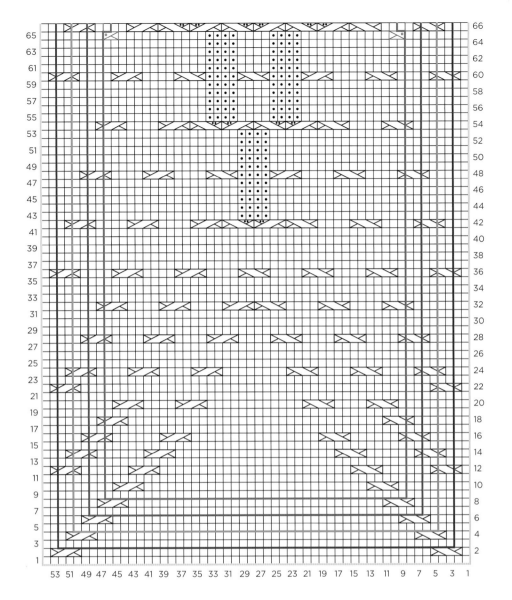

CHART NOTES

1. Work your size as indicated by the colored outlines.

2. Decreases are shaded in the color corresponding to the size being worked. Work only the decreases for your size.

KEY

☐	Knit on RS, purl on WS.
⊡	Purl on RS, knit on WS.
⧅	Slip 2 sts to cn, hold to back, k2, k2 from cn.
⧄	Slip 2 sts to cn, hold to front, k2, k2 from cn.
⧅	Slip 2 sts to cn, hold to back, k2, p2 from cn.
⧄	Slip 2 sts to cn, hold to front, p2, k2 from cn.
⧄	P2tog tbl
⧄	P2tog
☐	Size Petite
☐	Size Small
☐	Size Medium
☐	Size Large
☐	Size X-Large

FINISHING

Sew all Gores to each other along shaping edge. *Waistband:* Using circ needle, pick up and knit 22 (26, 30, 34, 38) sts along top edge of each Gore—132 (156, 180, 204, 228) sts. Join for working in the rnd, being careful not to twist sts; place marker (pm) for beginning of rnd. Begin 2×2 Rib. Work even for 7". BO all sts in pattern. Fold Waistband in half to outside. *Bottom Edging:* Using circ needle, pick up and knit 36 (40, 44, 48, 52) sts along bottom edge of each Gore—216 (240, 264, 288, 312) sts. Join for working in the rnd, being careful not to twist sts; place marker (pm) for beginning of rnd. Purl 1 rnd. Knit 1 rnd. BO all sts purlwise.

EASY SKIRT

GORES (make 6)

CO 38 (42, 46, 50, 54) sts; begin St st. Work even until piece measures 19 ¾ (20 ½, 21, 21 ¾, 22 ¼)" working decreases as indicated on Chart—24 (28, 32, 36, 40) sts. BO all sts knitwise.

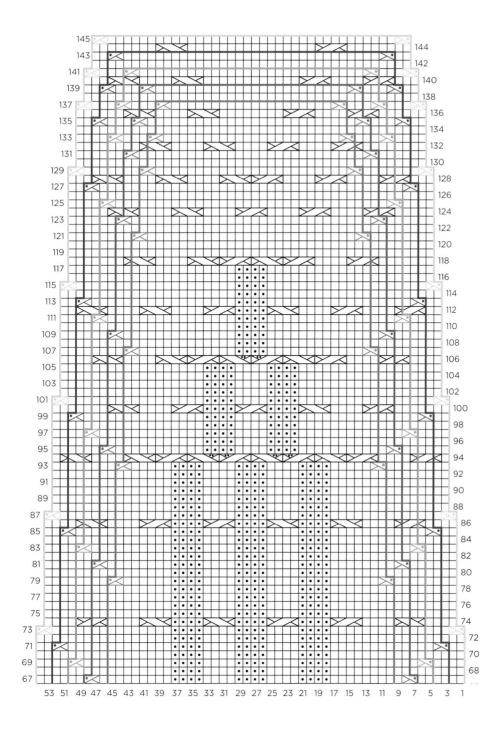

FINISHING

Note: Refer to chart for decreases only. Skirt is work entirely in St st. Sew all Gores to each other along shaping edge, with seam to outside. ***Waistband:*** WS facing, using smaller needles, pick up and knit 22 (26, 30, 34, 38) sts along top edge of each Gore—132 (156, 180, 204, 228) sts. Join for working in the rnd, being careful not to twist sts; place marker (pm) for beginning of rnd. Begin 2×2 Rib. Work even for 7". BO all sts in pattern. Fold Waistband in half to outside. ***Bottom Edging:*** Using crochet hook, work 1 rnd Sl st along bottom edge of each Gore. Work 1 rnd reverse sc. ***Seam Finishing:*** Using crochet hook, work 1 row sc along all seams and Waistband pick up row.

YARN
Tahki Yarns Donegal Tweed
Homespun (100% pure new wool; 138
yards/100 grams): 1 hank #824 sage

NEEDLES
One pair straight needles size US 6
(4 mm)

One pair straight needles size US 8
(5 mm)

Change needle size if necessary to
obtain correct gauge.

GAUGE
18 sts and 23 rows = 4" (10 cm) in
Stockinette st (St st) using larger
needles

STITCH PATTERNS
3×1 Rib:
(multiple of 4 sts + 2; 2-row repeat)
Row 1 (RS): *K1-tbl, p3; repeat from *
to last 2 sts, k1-tbl, p1.
Row 2: K1, p1, *K3, p1; repeat from *
to end.
Repeat Rows 1 and 2 for 3×1 Rib.

1×1 Rib:
(multiple of 2 sts; 1-row repeat)
All Rows: *K1, p1; repeat from * to
end.

Droplet Hat

This design is based upon a photo showing a droplet of water speeding downward propelled by gravity, spewing off little droplets as well as a narrow trail of water. My interpretation is rendered in bobbles and embossed leaves.

I don't like turning my knitting around to make bobbles, and I've never perfected knitting backwards. So, a few years ago I devised my own method of making no-turn bobbles, which is presented in this pattern.

NOTES

❱ **Stitch Patterns:** see left.

❱ **Bobble:** [K1-f/b] twice in next st to increase to 4 sts, slip these sts purlwise to left-hand needle with yarn in back, p4, slip these sts to left-hand needle with yarn in back, k4, slip third, second, and first sts one at a time over fourth st.

HAT

Using smaller needles, CO 94 sts; purl 2 rows. (RS) Begin 3×1 Rib. Work even for 4 rows. (RS) Bobble Row: *K1-tbl, p1, make bobble (mb), p1; repeat from * to last 2 sts, k1-tbl, k1. Work in 1×1 Rib for 3 rows. (RS) Change to larger needles and purl 1 row, decreasing 2 sts across row—92 sts remain. Knit 1 row.

Shape Hat:

Row 1 (RS): P1, *p6, p2tog, [(k1, yo) 4 times, k1] in next st to increase to 9 sts, p2tog, p 7; repeat from * to last st, p1—122 sts.

Row 2 and all WS Rows: Knit the knit sts and purl the purl sts as they face you.

Rows 3, 5 and 7: P1, *p7, k9, p8; repeat from * to last st, p1.

Row 9: P1, *p4, mb, p2, ssk, k5, k2tog, p2, mb, p 5; repeat from * to last st, p1—112 sts remain.

Row 11: P1, *p7, ssk, k3, k2tog, p8; repeat from * to last st, p1—102 sts remain.

Row 13: P1, *p7, ssk, k1, k2tog, p8; repeat from * to last st, p1—92 sts remain.

Row 15: P1, *p4, mb, p2, slip 2 sts tog as if to k2tog, k1, p2sso, p2, mb, p4, k1; repeat from * to last st, p1—82 sts remain.

Row 17: P1, *p7, k1; repeat from * to last st, p1.

Row 19: P1, p2tog, p5, k1, *p6, slip 2 sts tog as if to k2tog, k1, p2sso, p6, k1; repeat from * to last 9 sts, p6, k2tog, p1—72 sts remain.

Row 21: P1, *p3, mb, p2, k1, p2, mb, p3, k1; repeat from * to last st, p1.

Row 23: P1, *p5, slip 2 sts tog as if to k2tog, k1, p2sso, p5, k1; repeat from * to last st, p1—62 sts remain.

Row 25: P1, p2tog, p3, k1, *p4, slip 2 sts tog as if to k2tog, k1, p2sso, p4, k1; repeat from * to last 7 sts, p4, k2tog, p1—52 sts remain.

Row 27: P1, p2tog, *mb, p1, k1, p1, mb, p1, slip 2 sts tog as if to k2tog, k1, p2sso, p1; repeat from * to last 9 sts, mb, p1, k1, p1, mb, p1, k2tog, p1—42 sts remain.

Row 29: P1, *p2, slip 2 sts tog as if to k2tog, k1, p2sso, p2, k1; repeat from * to last st, p1—32 sts remain.

Row 31: P1, p2tog, *k1, p1, slip 2 sts tog as if to k2tog, k1, p2sso, p1; repeat from * to last 5 sts, k1, p1, k2tog, p1—22 sts remain.

Row 33: P1, *k2tog; repeat from * to last st, p1—12 sts remain.

Purl 1 row. Break yarn, thread through remaining sts, pull tight and fasten off. Sew seam.

ABBREVIATIONS

BO Bind off

Circ Circular

CO Cast on

Ch Chain

Dcd (double centered decrease) Slip next 2 sts together knitwise to right-hand needle, k1, pass 2 slipped sts over knit stitch.

Dpn Double-pointed needle(s)

K Knit

K2tog Knit 2 sts together.

K3tog Knit 3 sts together.

K1-f/b Knit into front loop and back loop of same stitch to increase one stitch.

Mb Make bobble (as instructed).

M1 With the tip of the left-hand needle inserted from front to back, lift the strand between the two needles onto the left-hand needle; knit the strand through the back loop to increase one stitch.

P Purl

P1-f/b Purl the next st through the front of its loop, then through the back of its loop, to increase one st.

Pm Place marker

Psso (pass slipped stitch over) Pass slipped st on right-hand needle over the sts indicated in the instructions, as in binding off.

P2sso (pass 2 slipped stitches over) Same as psso, but worked with 2 slipped sts.

Rnd Round

RS Right side

Sc Single crochet

Sl (slip) Slip stitch(es) as if to purl, unless otherwise specified.

Sl st (crochet slip stitch) Insert hook in st, yarn over hook, and draw through loop on hook.

Sm Slip marker

Ssk (slip, slip, knit) Slip next 2 sts to right-hand needle one at a time as if to knit; return them back to left-hand needle one at a time in their new orientation; knit them together through the back loop(s).

Sssk Same as ssk, but worked on next 3 sts.

Ssp (slip, slip, purl) Slip next 2 sts to right-hand needle one at a time as if to knit; return them to left-hand needle one at a time in their new orientation; purl them together through the back loop(s).

St(s) Stitch(es)

K1-tbl Knit one stitch through the back loop, twisting the stitch.

Tbl through the back loop

Tog Together

WS Wrong side

Wyib With yarn in back

Wyif With yarn in front

Yo Yarnover

YARN SOURCES

Adrienne Vittadini
JCA Inc.
35 Scales La.
Townsend, MA 01469
978-597-8794
www.jcacrafts.com

Berroco
14 Elmdale Rd.
P.O. Box 367
Uxbridge, MA 01569
508-278-2527
www.berroco.com

Classic Elite Yarns
122 Western Ave.
Lowell, MA 01851
978-453-2837
www.classiceliteyarns.com

Goddess Yarns
Redcoat La.
Little Rock, AR 72227
866-332-9276
www.goddessyarns.com

Harrisville Yarns
Center Village
P.O. Box 806
Harrisville, NH 03450
800-338-9415
www.harrisville.com

Jade Sapphire Exotic Fibers
148 Germonds Rd.
West Nyack, NY 10994
888-430-1674
www.jadesapphire.com

Jaeger
Westminster Fibers
4 Townsend West, Unit 8
Nashua, NH 03063
800-445-9276
wfibers@aol.com

Jo Sharp
JCA, Inc. (see Adrienne Vittadini)

Lang (see Berroco)

Manos del Uruguay
Design Source
P.O. Box 770
Medford, MA 02155
888-566-9970

One World Button Supply Co.
41 Union Square West
Suite 311
New York, NY 10003
www.oneworldbuttons.com

Reynolds
JCA Inc (see Adrienne Vittadini)

Rowan
Westminster Fibers (see Jaegar)

Tahki/Stacy Charles, Inc.
70-30 80th Street
Building 36
Ridgewood, NY 11385
800-338-9276
www.tahkistacycharles.com

Wendy (see Berroco)

RECOMMENDED READING

Ball, Phillip
The Self-Made Tapestry:
Pattern Formation in Nature
(Oxford University Press)

❱ *A great overview of patterns in nature and the science behind them, this book gave me the idea for* Knitting Nature.

Christie, Archibald H.
Pattern Design: An Introduction to the Study of Formal Ornament
(Dover)

❱ *It's well worth skimming through this overly scholarly and old-fashioned treatise to get to the sequential illustrations showing building complexity of pattern.*

Gleck, James
Chaos
(Penguin)

❱ *An introduction to fractal mathematics full of illustrations of interesting fractal shapes.*

Thompson, D'Arcy Wentworth
On Growth and Form
(Dover)

❱ *This old classic (first published in 1942) is still read by physicists and architects alike as an introduction to patterns in nature.*

Walker, Barbara
A Treasury of Knitting Patterns
(Schoolhouse Press)

❱ *The first in a series of three encyclopedic stitch dictionaries.*

Wolfram, Stephen
A New Kind of Science
(Wolfram Media Inc.)

❱ *This huge, dense volume explores the new science of explaining nature and physics mathematically in charted form. There are some very interesting sections on fractals, phyllotaxis, and other patterns from nature.*

Zimmermann, Elizabeth
Knitting Without Tears
(Scribners)

❱ *My love for designing knitwear began when I read this book as a teenager.*

ACKNOWLEDGMENTS

owe thanks to many people for helping me to make this book a reality. First I'd like to thank Joan and Merrit Heminway, Amy Mackenzie, Barb Rolnick and Nate Blum, and John and Helena Scholand, who although not avid knitters themselves, have lavished support and encouragement upon me since the beginning of my career. Thanks to Janet D'Alesandre, Claire Atwell, Ruth Sunn, Pat Slaven, and Lily Decarlo, comrades in knitting who have been like family over the years—been there to lend an ear, helping hand, or a good dinner. Thanks to Grace Judson for teaching me how to knit. Thanks to Margery Winter for being a great mentor and thanks to Milo Winter for putting up with us.

During the writing of this book I relied on the sample knitters not only to knit the garments, but to patiently and intelligently catch the problems with my original instructions as well. Thanks for your invaluable help: Claire Atwell, Dottie Barr, Noreen Blood, Papatya Curtis, Janet D'Alesandre, Maria Drayne, Claire Herne, June Metta, Karin Morin, Ann Parks, and Fran Scullin. I am stunned and amazed by the talents brought to this book by Thayer Gowdy's photography and Karen Schaupeter's styling. I am grateful for the patience and persistence of my editor, Melanie Falick, for helping me to make my thoughts clear. Many thanks to Sue McCain for rising to the challenge of pattern-editing the unorthodox shapes contained herein. And thanks to Anna Christian for her gorgeous graphic design. Thanks again to Mom for years and years of love and support as well as the illustrations for this volume. Special thanks to John Ranta for research, for computer help, for amazement, for being there. Finally, thanks to Phillip Ball for writing *The Self-Made Tapestry*, the science book that triggered this project and that I referred back to so many times.

INDEX